SHANGHAI ACROBAT

SHANGHAI ACROBAT

A True Story of Courage and
Perseverance from Revolutionary China

JINGJING XUE

TRANSLATED BY BO AI

APOLLO
PUBLISHERS

Shanghai Acrobat: A True Story of Courage
and Perseverance from Revolutionary China
Copyright © 2021 by Jingjing Xue and Malcolm Knox

All rights reserved. No part of this book may be used or reproduced
in any manner whatsoever without the written permission of the
publisher, except in the case of brief excerpts in critical reviews or
articles. All inquiries should be sent by email to Apollo Publishers
at info@apollopublishers.com. Apollo Publishers books may be
purchased for educational, business, or sales promotional use.
Special editions may be made available upon request. For details,
contact Apollo Publishers at info@apollopublishers.com.

Visit our website at www.apollopublishers.com.

Translated from Chinese by Bo Ai.
Published by arrangement with Black, Inc.

Published in compliance with California's Proposition 65.

Library of Congress Control Number: 2020942965

Print ISBN: 978-1-948062-74-9
Ebook ISBN: 978-1-948062-75-6

Printed in the United States of America.

CONTENTS

To my parents, for whom I am still searching.
I love you always.

PRELUDE

IN THE ANCIENT LAND OF China there is a legend that, among all the animals who are born into this world, only humans cry. Every infant bears a birthmark on their back: the footprint of Yan Wang, the King of Hell, from when he forcefully kicked the child out into the world. Babies cry about the endless ocean of bitterness and suffering that awaits them there.

According to the legend, all people, wealthy or poor, noble or otherwise, have to endure lifelong suffering on their own. Some believe the legend and some don't, but it contains some of humankind's biggest philosophical questions: Where did I come from? What do I live for? Why am I here? Where am I going? What is the meaning of my life?

From infancy, we were told old legends such as this, all of which had some bearing on our modern lives. It was important to know our place, so another Chinese legend we learned was that humanity is divided into three types: those who are immovable, those who are movable and those who move on their own. Those who move invent theories, those who are movable propagate these theories and those who are immovable accept them. For thousands of years, the movers—philosophers who ponder, explore and answer timeless questions—have set up their schools of thought. The movable help spread these philosophies. The immovable, baffled by all these ideas, can only find one explanation for what happens in their lives: destiny. Destiny can be neither altered nor foretold. It dictates our lives and cannot be controlled.

A humble soul in this vast universe, I was taught that I belong to the third class, the immovables. However, I'm a little bit different. I believe there is destiny, but I refuse to succumb to it. Even though I am a lonely sailor on the endless ocean of suffering, faced with strong winds and huge waves, I sail persistently toward the far shore.

1

THE CHOSEN

You! ... You! ... Not you. ... *You!*"

The man was moving through the rows of students, coming toward me. I did not know whether I wanted him to choose me or not, as I had no idea where his decision might lead.

"You!"

He was getting closer. I shivered, but forced back the urge to stamp my feet. I was nine years old and this place, the Youth Village, was the fifth orphanage I had lived in. It was by far the worst. The classroom, where we were standing in lines waiting for this strange man to inspect us, was on the first floor of a red brick building facing west, receiving no sun until late in the day—and for most of the year. Sometimes, we children were allowed outside between classes to find a pool of sunlight to bathe in for a few precious minutes. Mostly, we froze in the below-freezing Shanghai temperatures. When it got too cold to bear, the older students would begin to stamp their feet and we would watch the teacher for his reaction. If he said nothing, we would all copy the older students. Once, in a rare show of sympathy, the teacher stopped the class and let us keep stamping until we warmed up.

"You!"

He was close to me now. All we had been told was that he had come from the Shanghai Acrobatic Troupe, which was said to be famous, but I had no idea what an acrobatic troupe did, or what "famous" meant.

The man from the troupe, with one of our teachers beside him, stopped in front of me. He did not touch me, but merely swept his eyes over my body. I was the smallest child in the class. I had been an orphan since I was two years old.

"*You!*"

⸱ ⸱ ⸱

Three weeks passed before the man came back. In the meantime, we went about our normal routines in the Youth Village. The main building, a red brick former church, was our dining and meeting hall. Another red brick building, forming an L with the hall, contained dormitories for boys on the ground floor, with girls a floor above. My dormitory was jam-packed with bunk beds for more than twenty boys, from nine to sixteen years of age. The air was thick with smelly feet and farts. In the dining hall we ate plain flour noodles, cooked in soup with bran, pumpkins and carrots, without any trace of meat. Hunger was constant, as was constipation. Our hopes rose when the older boys wrote a petition to request better food, but nothing came of it. If those strong older boys could achieve nothing on such an essential matter, we were all powerless.

At the end of the L-shaped building complex, next to a wall connected to the main gate of the former church, was a dirt basketball court, where in the mornings we did exercises and at dusk we played. Sometimes we flew kites, and occasionally, against the wall of this court, there would be screenings of Russian war movies such as *Lenin in October* and *Chapaev,* the favorites of the older boys, who rushed to occupy the front rows. Those boys were like my big brothers and looked after me, but after everything I had been through already, I had developed a very independent character.

I had been chosen, but for what? While I waited to find out, I learned more about the Shanghai Acrobatic Troupe. Before "liberation"—the word we were taught to use for the Communist revolution that had taken control of China seven years earlier, in 1949—acrobats, or "trick-players," were from the lowest stratum of society. Only those families who could not make a living would send their children to an acrobatic troupe to learn "tricks," in the hope that they would have a trade to support themselves. After liberation, the status of acrobats sank even lower. Finding students became so difficult, the Shanghai Acrobatic Troupe had to turn to the orphanages.

Three weeks after that initial visit, I was told to report to the Teaching Affairs Office, where I found myself among a group of boys and girls aged from nine to fourteen. More people from the troupe had come with the man who had done the original selection.

"Stand still!"

Another man held a tape measure at my head and along my arms and legs.

"Jump!"

I jumped.

"Grip as hard as you can!"

I gripped as hard as I could.

"Show the arch of your foot!"

I showed him the arches of my feet.

"Let me see your face!"

I did my best to show the recruiters a pleasing face.

Nobody explained why they were doing each test. No one asked us whether we wanted to learn acrobatics, or what our interests and hobbies were. This was just a measurement process, as if we were livestock being sized up. But for what? We were not told, yet when they ordered us back to our dormitories to pack up our meagre belongings, we were just happy that we could leave. No place could be as bad as the Youth Village. And I knew how bad the orphanages of Shanghai could be.

2

LEFT

Eleven years earlier, in 1945, Imperial Japan's eight-year occupation of China came to an end. The joyful sound of firecrackers gave way in 1946 to a new wave of fighting, as the Chinese Communist Party and the Kuomintang, or Chinese Nationalist Party, resumed the civil war that had been interrupted by the Japanese invasion.

One year after the civil war restarted, I was born in a beautiful little town near Ningbo, Zhejiang Province. My family, who in typical Chinese fashion valued boys much more than girls, gathered to watch me protesting loudly at my arrival. They cheered and laughed. But I cried as if I knew what was ahead of me.

Ningbo, a major port city, lies ninety miles south of Shanghai across Hangzhou Bay. A trading post on the Silk Road for thousands of years, Ningbo established its seaport during the Tang dynasty, in the seventh century AD. The city became rich in goods and produce, exporting crafts and food, and became a center of learning and scholarship. After the British defeated the Qing dynasty in the first Opium War in 1842, imposing the Treaty of Nanking, Ningbo, along with four other ports, was opened to the West. While its northern neighbor Shanghai quickly developed into China's first modern city and economic center, Ningbo fell behind.

For people from Ningbo, Shanghai represented a vibrant dream, an opportunity to change their destiny. Rich families sent their children to Shanghai for a good education; poor families tried to arrange for their children to learn a trade. Some poor families even had their children adopted in Shanghai to give them a better future. The people in Ningbo were very pragmatic in the face of misfortune. During the Second World War, Japan dropped ceramic bombs filled with fleas infected with bubonic plague on Ningbo.

In late 1949, when I traveled from Ningbo to Shanghai by ship, I knew nothing of this history. I was only two but that day was such a turning point in my life, it engraved itself on my memory. I still vividly remember how windy it was. The waves became so big that our boat rocked not only up and down but sideways. In the stuffy lower cabin, I became seasick. I vomited and cried and made a scene. In my memory, my uncle, who was in his early twenties, was only a bigger boy, and did not know how to look after a toddler. He was seasick too. I remember him clumsily holding me tight, letting me cry.

On our arrival in Shanghai, Uncle took me to visit relatives. They received us with much hospitality, but none was willing to take me in. In the end, in early 1950 he took me to an orphanage. On the way, he sighed and said: "Do you know, you brought such great joy to the family. On the day you were born, all gathered around you. Everyone said, 'Great. It's a boy.' But, now ...."

He couldn't finish, and fell silent for the rest of the journey. He took me to the Fuyou Orphanage in the southern suburbs of Shanghai near the Huangpu River. All my life I have asked myself why he did this, why my relatives would not take me in, and what my parents back in Ningbo thought was happening to me. Was an orphan's life what they wanted for me?

We entered the orphanage through a broad gate of thick wood with peeling black paintwork. Behind it was a two-story traditional residential building of gray bricks and black tiles. In front was a small courtyard, covered in gray cement, and behind it was a dirty playground. Inside, the timber floorboards squeaked with each step we took. Apart from the shiny railings in the corridor, everything—the walls, the ceilings, the doors, the windows and the timber boards—was dark gray. Even the parts exposed to the sun did not show much life. The kitchen and dining hall, to the side of the courtyard, looked newer than the main building. A tall slim man wearing reading glasses and an old changshan, the traditional tunic worn by Chinese men, received us in his shabby office. His name was Wang Ying.

After a brief discussion, which I didn't follow, Uncle turned and left. Only then did it dawn on me, very vaguely, that my uncle was abandoning me in this strange place. Engulfed with fear, I rushed after him, but the black gate was pulled shut behind him. I kicked and banged heavily on the wood, crying in despair. I tried to fight off the teachers who were holding me back. I struggled and wept; no one could calm me down. I lost my voice. In the end, exhausted, I fell asleep, still weeping. I remember all of this.

The moment I walked through the Fuyou Orphanage gate, my life was changed for the worse. I would never see my father, my mother or my other relatives again.

When I woke the next morning, I found myself in a bed, sharing a room with several other children. Destiny had brought us all here. Apart from eating and sleeping, we spent our time in the courtyard and corridors playing hide-and-seek. Without any toys, we found ways to entertain ourselves, as children do: we crouched and watched ants moving house, or we watched birds flying past the small patch of sky visible above the courtyard.

With playmates and an ability to adapt to a strange new environment, I got used to living in the Fuyou Orphanage. But I was still a boy under three, and needed the care and warmth of a family and the love of parents. I became a wounded cub who could only lick his wounds in silence, and struggle to survive.

In 1950, when I was three, I fell down the stairs, hit my head against some stones and had to be taken to hospital for stitches. After coming back from the hospital, with a dressing around my head, I sat near the gate, looking at it with expectant eyes. Now I had been hurt, surely my uncle would show up! No matter how discouraging the other boys were, I sat and waited in silence, watching the dilapidated gate, willing my uncle to come through it.

Eventually, an older boy walked over and said, "Don't wait like a fool. When your family sent you here, they didn't think about taking you back. Don't dream anymore. We are all in the same boat."

I didn't listen to him. I firmly believed my uncle would come and take me home. I can still feel the desperate longing as if it were yesterday.

My family had never let me starve, nor had they left me out in the cold. What had happened to them? Why would my parents abandon me to an orphanage? It was all too much of a mystery for a three-year-old to understand.

Later that year, I suffered a second setback when I came down with pneumonia, which developed into tuberculosis. I was so sick that I vomited blood. The director and founder of Fuyou Orphanage, Dong Bin, dispatched me to Renji Hospital, a church hospital, and paid for my care and medications, including numerous shots of penicillin. A couple of months later, I finally recovered. Tuberculosis had a high fatality rate, and were it not for Mr. Dong's help, which must have cost him a lot of money, that could have been the last chapter of my life.

Mr. Dong had become a person of importance to me, but when I returned from the hospital, his office was closed with police seals that I couldn't read. I learned that he had been arrested on the charge of raping an underage girl. Too young to understand properly, I only felt great fear and loneliness, and his disappearance brought back the emotions of losing my uncle. I panicked, wondering, who is going to look after me now?

I, among other orphans from Fuyou, was transferred to Xin Puyu Tang, an orphanage established by a British church, in 1952. The red brick buildings looked beautiful. Nearly a hundred children slept in a few big rooms, with one nanny looking after us. The ground floor was used as classrooms. Next door was a small church from which we often heard the organ being played. Christian churches were still permitted in China then, and every day I saw black-robed foreign priests and Chinese and foreign nuns wearing white. Services and masses were held in a small chapel.

Orphans were not required to be baptized or to attend the services, but I went with the older children. In the orphanages, older children would traditionally look after the younger ones, but we would never address each other as brother or sister. I was the smallest child in Xin Puyu Tang, and I was cute, so the older ones liked to play with me and take me wherever they went.

I was fascinated by the religious atmosphere in the church. The choir and organ music took me to a mysterious heavenly kingdom. As for what the priest was saying, I had no idea. I didn't know what the holy bread we ate represented. I simply followed what the older boys were doing.

Before entering the church, everyone was required to kneel on one knee, dip their fingers in the holy water and make the sign of a cross.

I asked an older boy, "Is the holy water tap water?"

He looked at me disdainfully and said, "Stop your nonsense."

I never did find out where the holy water came from.

There was a religious atmosphere inside the orphanage, too. Nuns would walk around holding Bibles, from which they would recite. The standards by which they judged everything came from this book. The most discussed question was: When a person dies, on the day of the Last Judgement, will they go to Heaven or to Hell? I was very afraid of discussions of death, and found a few terrifying phrases about the Last Judgement hard to delete from my mind.

The church had been the site of a miracle involving a statue of the Virgin Mary. Just prior to the Second World War, when the Japanese air force was dropping bombs on Shanghai, one fell toward the orphanage. The Virgin Mary was said to have used her hand to block the bomb and save the orphanage. I heard this story from the senior students. As a boy of five, I didn't understand what a Japanese plane, or a bomb, was. However, whenever I walked past the Virgin Mary, I would look up at her with great awe.

It was in that church that I first encountered art. The parishioners received an Our Lady medal, which seemed precious and desirable to me, and I loved to gaze at the colorful stained-glass windows with Biblical figures. On Christmas Eve, the church was lit up with candles that glistened like stars in the sky. The ceremony that night, the songs and the nativity play imbued the heart and soul of each person with religious warmth and beauty.

On Christmas Day, every orphan woke up to find a small bag containing gifts. The teacher told us it was left by Santa Claus, who had come in the night on a sleigh drawn by reindeers. I couldn't imagine the scene the teacher was describing, but the small pack of sweets felt like a gift from Heaven. It was my first taste of candy. Both the Christmas Eve ceremony and the gift from Santa were unforgettable. Alas, a year after my arrival, the Chinese Communist

Party, which was now in complete control of the country, banned Christianity and shut down the churches. The ban took some years to take full effect, with orphanages being closed progressively.

To the other side of our orphanage was a cow shed. Whenever I went past, a pungent odor would assail my nostrils. Just the same, I liked to watch the huge, relaxed animals eating grass. Once, I saw a cow giving birth to a calf. When later on I came across the phrase "the affection of a cow licking her calf," I remembered I had seen it with my own eyes, and it moved me deeply.

As dictated by the British mission schools' system, I started school at the age of five, in 1952. The textbooks were published by the Chinese government, and there were no religious workers among the teaching staff. I enjoyed school. I liked the sounds of students reading aloud, the fragrance of the ink from the newly printed books, and the pictures and diagrams in them. The teacher's calligraphy on the blackboard was also art to me. Whenever I learned a new character, whenever I was able to work out a calculation, I was filled with joy. The classes eased my loneliness and gave me a new lease on life.

During one afternoon class, a teacher from the coordinator's office came and asked me to go with her.

"Why do you want to see me in your office?" I asked her.

"Your mother has come to see you."

In the two years since Uncle had left me at Fuyou Orphanage, no one had ever come to visit me, and I was slow to react.

"Who has come to see me?"

"Your mother."

This should have sent me into ecstasies, but I was too stunned to get my head around the idea.

"Who?"

"It's your mother." The teacher was very firm in her tone.

Occasionally parents, Chinese or foreign, did come and collect their children. Those families had been separated by war. Whenever I saw orphans being collected by their parents, I wished I could be the lucky one. And it seemed it was now my turn. My mom had come to collect me! As the shock subsided, my heart raced. I would have a home and live with my parents, like other children! I would say goodbye to this place where I didn't belong.

I had left home so young that I couldn't remember what my mom looked like. I had conjured up an image using a jigsaw puzzle of faces from movies and pictures, and even my female teachers. In my imagination, my mom was kind and she loved me very much. When she saw me, she would hug me as affectionately as the cows tended their calves, and she would use her warm palms to touch my face. How I had longed for this moment. The mom I had called for millions of times in my heart—I was about to see her! I would be able to call her "Mom" to her lovely face. I could feel my heart thumping stronger and stronger, my face turning hotter and hotter; sweat broke out on my forehead. I skipped all the way to the office, not a long distance, but it seemed endless that day.

When I got there, I saw a woman standing by the door in a Lenin-style military uniform and faded cloth shoes. She was not wearing a military cap, and her hair was short. Her face was kind.

The teacher pointed at her.

"She's your mother."

I looked at her blankly. She returned my gaze compassionately. When she looked into my eyes, I felt nothing. Absolutely nothing. I was certain, there and then, without the shadow of a doubt, that this was not her. Even now, I don't know why I was so sure.

The woman began to speak of many things about our "home," but she didn't mention my uncle, who was her brother. My instinct about her felt more correct with every word she spoke, and I realized that she wanted to adopt a child. I had learned of this word—"adoption"—from the other, older boys. I wanted to leave desperately, but only to be with my own parents. I couldn't go to another family. It might get me out of the orphanage, but it would surely end any hopes I still had of being reunited with my true family. A warning voice kept repeating in my ears: Don't go with her! Don't go with her!

"You are not my mom," I told her. "I'm not going with you."

"Why do you think that? I AM your mother. When you left home, you were too little to remember. You are not to be blamed. In time, when we get to know each other, you'll see I am telling the truth. You must come with me now."

She was trying to trick me.

"No. I'm not going with you," I insisted.

"We have investigated. You are her child." The teacher was on her side.

The more they persisted, the less I believed them, and we found ourselves in a deadlock.

As a last resort, the teacher suggested, "Let's check the birthmark."

Checking birthmarks is a traditional way of identifying a biological son or daughter. When families tried to find their children after becoming separated during the Communist revolution, the location of the birthmark was the first question they were asked. The older children at the orphanage had warned me never to say where my birthmark was, to prevent anyone wanting to adopt me from pretending to be my parent. Knowing, from those older boys, exactly where my birthmark was—on the back of my left shoulder-blade—was priceless secret information. The teacher and the woman in the Lenin suit both thought I wouldn't know where my birthmark was, and believed that they could just randomly say a spot and I would believe them. They were wrong. When my self-proclaimed mother announced, in a matter-of-fact manner, the supposed location of my birthmark—on my back—I knew I was right about her. To prove she was not my mom, I undressed and showed them the mark on my shoulderblade, where Yan Wang the King of Hell had kicked me out into this world.

The mother-son reunion ended there. The woman left in great disappointment. I stood next to the teacher, watching her walk out of the orphanage. I remembered the moment my uncle disappeared behind the gate at Fuyou. Suddenly, the image of the two doors of the orphanage closing doubled me over in pain.

She never returned. If she really was my mother, she would have kept coming back until I changed my mind. The painful truth was that even though I had denied she was my mom, I had wished so much that she was, and that I could go home with her, to be with my relatives.

Like a river, life will not stop at one place. A few months later, the orphanage was closed without warning or explanation and I was transferred yet again, to St. Joseph's orphanage, and from there to the Good Shepherd. These two orphanages, both established by foreign churches, had good conditions for living and studying. I never knew why I was moved. An adult would just appear one day and tell us to pack.

The Good Shepherd orphanage was the better one, located in Xujiahui, the best district in Shanghai. Its iron gateway opened onto a wide tree-lined path. At the end was a three-story European-style building and a garden with a pond with tadpoles swimming in it. Green lawns extended to the walls, along which roses were planted. After 1953, the Good Shepherd could no longer operate as a church orphanage. No more religious celebrations, no preaching of the Holy Bible. It was only on Fridays when fish was served that I was reminded that it used to be part of a church. I liked the music lessons. Music is joyful, and relaxing, inspiring everyone with a longing for beauty.

There was a song which went: "Old yellow cow, big and fat. You came to my home after the Land Reform." This song was about a young boy herding cows, and it touched me because I was a similar age and felt a connection with these gentle animals. Unfortunately, after 1956, when the Communist government's collectivization movement peaked and private ownership of livestock was abolished, the song became outdated.

The Good Shepherd was a peaceful bay where I was able to temporarily avoid gusts and storms. However, storms sometimes strike even in peaceful waters. I remember one day, in a music class, we learned a patriotic Mongolian song, "My Motherland," the lyrics of which were composed by the poet Dashdorjiin Natsagdorj.

Every family is filled with happiness
Ha ha ha, filled with endless happiness . . . .

Each word was a dagger in my heart, reopening the wound where time had been forming a scar. Oh god, why were we made to sing such songs? The whole class felt the same. We were like eggplant seedlings that had just survived the early morning frost, only to be defeated now. The music teacher had to play the interlude several times and wondered why we still could not pick it up with the correct timing.

The Good Shepherd was not far from the Heng Shan Cinema, where the teachers took us to watch documentaries. Tickets were very cheap. Even though the documentaries were mostly about the Chinese National Day parade, I enjoyed sitting on the soft chairs. I had been in orphanages for four years, and these cinema trips were the first time I had been on an excursion for pleasure outside a main gate. Walking on the street, seeing all the vehicles, bicycles, tricycles and pedestrians, hearing the hawkers yelling outside the cinema, I felt the sharp differences between the worlds outside and inside the orphanage. I burned with envy when I saw a mother buy a pack of sweets and place it into the hands of a child my age. After returning to the Good Shepherd, I immersed myself in recollections of the scenes I had experienced.

In 1955, I, along with hundreds of children from orphanages that had been shut down during the banning of the churches, was transferred to the Youth Village. If life in the Good Shepherd was light blue in color, with a tinge of sweetness, then life in the Youth Village was dark gray and filled with bitterness. But it was my last orphanage. I was there for one year before the man came from the Shanghai Acrobatic Troupe.

3

A NEW DAWN

Shanghai in April was beautiful, with soft spring breezes and an azure sky. Nature was at her most vital, green and full of energy on the day when thirty of us from the Youth Village climbed into a truck to drive west across the city to the Shanghai Acrobatic Troupe's compound. On the truck, my brain went blank, as if I were in a fog. As the wheels turned, so did my destiny.

We turned into Central Yan'an Road, south of the bustling Nanjing Road, in the heart of the French Concession in Shanghai. The truck slowed down in front of the Moller residence, a grand villa built in 1936 by a Swedish shipbuilder who still operated his business there. This villa was where the government housed the troupe. Why? We didn't know. The Indian consulate was opposite our gate, and we saw turbaned, bearded Sikhs in Western clothing coming in and out on tricycles.

As we entered the walled compound, the first thing I saw was a three-story pebble dash and wood European-style building covered with climbing plants, next to a beautiful garden glowing with the greens and reds of Chinese ilex and winter plum. An old gardener worked among the flowers. I would learn that Uncle Ding, as the gardener was known, kept his mouth closed, hoping no one would connect him with his previous masters, a capitalist family who had fled Shanghai after liberation.

In front of this building was a small patch of lawn, with a cobblestone path leading to the southeast, where another world lay hidden. The winding path (like those seen in ancient Chinese paintings) led to a tranquil Chinese garden. At the entrance to this garden was a stone boat inscribed with four characters, Song Huang Shen Chu, or "In the Deep Pine Forest," by the famous artist Shen Yinmo. Past the stone boat, we could see a small bridge with little lions carved on it, and a pond with a fountain. Schools of goldfish swam among the lotus flowers, bringing the serene garden to life. Around the pond was a man-made mountain constructed out of rocks from Lake Tai Hu. On top of the rocks was a pavilion.

The compound had been adapted to suit the troupe's needs. They built a brick exercise building and a stage made from timber panels, dried reeds and iron pipes on the south lawn, in front of the spired European building. To the south of the exercise building was the dining hall. On the north, east and southern three sides of the Chinese garden, a shed had been built out of timber and asphaltic felt, a workshop for the carpenters and coppersmiths.

For our induction, we observed the acrobats in their daily drills. I was amazed to see people standing on their hands, doing loops and flips, bending their backs, and walking on a tightrope. My first knowledge of acrobatics had come from comic books—I remember in particular *Sanmao the Roamer (A Poor Boy's Stories)*, drawn by Zhang Leping. The hero, Sanmao, wanted to formally learn the "tricks" of a master from Shandong Province and, wearing a belt that strained his already slim waist, nearly broke his back attempting them. When Sanmao bent backward the picture suggested that he was undergoing extreme torture. I

Shanghai, 2004: The pavilion and the pond in the troupe's compound are still just as I remember them.

was horrified by the look on his face. At the time of reading the comic book, it never occurred to me that one day I might encounter this unusual form of punishment.

But here I was, among boys and girls from different backgrounds and places. The majority were children of members of the Kuomintang (KMT), the losing side in the civil war. Many KMT members and their families had retreated to Taiwan in 1949, but they left behind a vast number of military and administrative staff, most of whom were jailed by the Communist government. Their children were sent to orphanages, and a handful went on to this acrobatic troupe, where they became my classmates.

In the new China, class weighed heavily. Mao Zedong had said, "In a class society, everyone has a certain status, all kinds of ideas are marked with the stigma of class." Hence, we entered the world not only with a foot-shaped birthmark from the King of Hell, but also with an ineradicable label of social status. In a society where class struggle was the norm, children born to the wrong families were labeled counter-revolutionary. Compared with those KMT children, I was fortunate in terms of class, but we ended up in the same place, which shows how low I was as an orphan.

* * *

Starting in 1956, a five-year acrobatic program was taught at the troupe. The program broke the thousand-year-old Chinese tradition in which one master single-handedly taught his students, and replaced it with an educational scheme based on the Soviet model. Staff included professional acrobats, and cultural, dance and music teachers. We received training in all of these areas, laying the foundations for us to become skilled acrobats who would make our names throughout the world.

All costs for education, food and board were covered by the government. The food was vastly better than that at the orphanage. Whereas the orphanage fed us simply to keep us alive, the acrobatic school provided good nutrition to fuel our bodies for training and exercise. For breakfast we had rice porridge and buns with mince fillings, and lunch was various combinations of vegetables and meat, with unlimited rice. That was a rare thing in a country where food supply was controlled by the use of ration cards.

Separate dormitories for boys and girls were located in two big sunlit, airy rooms on the third floor of the pebble dash building. These rooms were also used as classrooms. We did not complain about the limited indoor space because we were happy having the garden with the rock mountain to roam in and play hide-and-seek.

Political education—inculcating revolutionary ideology into the minds of future proletarians—was the objective in class. The school day started with politics and history, which amounted to the same subject. Teacher Xu told us the history of the Shanghai Acrobatic Troupe. She said that in October 1950, Chairman Mao Zedong, Premier Zhou Enlai and other leaders viewed performances by the best acrobats in China and, based on that night's performance, Premier Zhou proposed that a national acrobatic troupe be founded. The name change from "trick-players" to "acrobats" was a first sign of improved status. The government saw a political use for us: this troupe, the first of its kind in China, had visited the Soviet Union and set a precedent for artistic groups to travel abroad to perform, spread the message of the new China and become an avenue for cultural exchange with the outside world.

Initially, the troupe had lacked good conditions and practice facilities. Members had to exercise outdoors, even when it was windy or raining. For aerial performances, the gear and equipment had to be fastened onto trees for safety. The exercise hall had been completed in 1954, a big improvement.

During the Korean War, when China fought against the United States to support North Korea, members of the troupe went to the battlefield three times and performed for the soldiers while under attack from American bombers and machine guns. Their bravery had a great political influence on the troupe. Through hard work and persistence, we had gained a good reputation nationwide and the majority of our members were performing in Romania, Hungary, Poland and East Germany, building friendships within the socialist world.

Xu asked us: "Class, are the conditions here good or not?"

"Gooooood!" we all replied loudly.

"Now, the country has provided the funding to train you. I hope all of you will take advantage of this opportunity to study here and become successful acrobats in the new China. At home, you will serve the workers, peasants and soldiers. When you go abroad, you will contribute your efforts to cultural exchange with foreign countries, and bring honor to our country. Class, do you have the confidence to do this?"

In the new China, being an acrobat was a good career. As long as we worked hard, we would have a great future. I was not sure whether I could be a successful acrobat, but I yelled out "Yes!" along with my excited classmates.

During the next class we watched a movie called *Acrobatic Performance on a Holiday,* about a troupe that had received an urgent notice on a Sunday to perform. Things became chaotic as everyone tried to return from their holiday in time. Eventually they all showed up and gave a perfect performance. We were amused by the funny storyline but, more powerfully, amazed by the excellent acrobatic performances.

The acrobatics I saw in this movie were totally different from those I knew from the comic books about Sanmao the Roamer. I had never before seen anyone do a handstand on a moving unicycle. My interest was aroused; I gained an inkling of the high level of skill required for international acrobatics. The movie inspired me in a way that nothing else ever had. It seemed that life here was going to be immeasurably better than in the orphanage—except in one important regard.

4

ENDURE!

Two days after our arrival, training officially started.

We rose at five-thirty for the morning's drill, from six to eleven-thirty. All basic training started with back flexibility, leg flexibility, handstands and tumbling. These were necessary exercises and had been passed down for many generations. Acrobats must be trained to have strength, flexibility, balance, dexterity and, most important of all, the strength of will that can only come with strenuous effort and learning from failure.

Our instructor, Li Dianqi, was a gentle man of medium height who walked with slow, small, deliberate steps. Everything he said was precise: "This is good. This is not good. Let me show you the right way."

He had been a very good acrobat, but during a performance he fell and suffered severe damage to his spine. Before he had fully recovered, he was sent to North Korea to perform for the Chinese soldiers fighting there. The acrobats had to live in cold, damp caves to avoid American air strikes and, because of those poor living conditions, he never entirely recovered. Unable to continue his career as an acrobat, he became an instructor.

The early morning drill started with handstands against the wall, to prepare us for being upside down for sustained periods and to build our arm strength. At the beginning, I felt all the blood in my body flow to my head. My face grew red, my breath shortened and my arms trembled violently. Li said, "Hold it, hold it!" Before he could say the third "Hold it," my arms gave way and my head banged on the ground. Even though the sound was loud, and it gave me quite a shock, I didn't feel any pain, as my head was already so close to the ground.

"Up you get. In position!"

In that first half-hour, I forget now how many times I had to repeat this. I could see others were going through the same hell. It was impossible for us to understand that it was these simple repetitive drills and endless failures that would eventually lead to success, and encourage the strong will of a fighter.

Every morning, we had one fear on our minds: that we might not finish our quota of ten sets of handstand drills, ten handstands in each. If we could only finish nine continuous handstands in one full set, we would be punished with another full set. The more punishment, the less we could complete our drills, so it was a vicious circle. By the end of each morning session, we were exhausted. Li would point at those who were being punished with more handstands, saying, "Don't be lazy! Complete your drill set and look up to those who can complete them as your models."

I felt lucky that I seemed to escape punishment more than some others. Li tried to make me understand the exercise and learn the correct skills. Then he increased the intensity of the drills in order to achieve a breakthrough from quantity to quality. It was his rigorous training approach that led me to choose the handstand as my main performance.

Years later, when I had achieved some success, I thanked Li

personally: "Without your initial thorough training, I would not be what I am today."

"I did not do that much," he said. "It was you who worked hard. I was only a teacher, with my professional ethics and my sense of justice."

These words became my motto when I chose to become a teacher. There is a Chinese saying: "A master will guide your way, but it is you who need to practice."

As a nine-year-old, however, I found the early morning training very hard, and while life in the troupe was an improvement on the Youth Village, it also presented new varieties of suffering. After drills I was always hungry and exhausted. Instead of washing my hands as required by the school, I would just rinse them, rub them dry on my trousers and rush to the canteen for breakfast. I was often stopped by the student guards on duty and made to wash my hands again before being allowed into the canteen. Breakfasts soon lost their savor. My hands, shaking from the repetitive handstand drills, could hardly hold the chopsticks and bowl, so I gulped down rice porridge, mince buns and preserved vegetables, stuffing myself until I belched.

After half an hour for breakfast, the morning drill went from eight to eleven-thirty. On the exercise ground, we were forced like a herd of sheep onto a long, single-plank bridge with nowhere to go but forward. Giving up was not an option, and nor could we stop to look around.

Because our stomachs were still digesting, the next class was leg flexibility exercises. Two rows of square-shaped wooden bars had been installed for this purpose. The higher bars were designed for girls, whose flexibility was better, with the lower row for boys. Acrobats can be classified into two types: the flexible type and the strong type. Very few are good in both areas. I am the strong type, and the flexibility exercises almost killed me! I was the youngest and shortest. When other boys stood near the bar and stretched out one leg, their leg would form a 90-degree angle, whereas I, being short, had to stretch to a 100-degree angle, and my knees would not straighten. Instructor Wong had to push my knees down, causing a searing pain to run through my body. Sweat would run down my forehead, and tears down my face.

"Clench your teeth. Don't cry! If you cry, I'll overstretch your legs again and more!" Wong would warn me, before going to do the same thing to another boy. When the time came to change legs, often both of mine had become numb and I could not move.

No sooner had we finally dragged ourselves through leg flexibility training class than we were thrown into more torture: back flexibility training. The objective was to force our backs to bend backward to form an arch, thereby softening our shoulders, back, waist and hips. When we are in our mother's womb, we crouch forward. Stretching backward is extremely hard for any of us. Wong would stand in front of me, with his knees against my knees, and bend me backward. I was afraid my back and waist would break, and the more I thought about it, the more painful it became.

Wong had been recruited from the Peking Opera troupe in Shanghai. He was big and tall, with a hot temper and a loud voice. We were all very afraid of him. When it came to verbal abuse, Wong was actually one of the gentler ones, speaking slowly and clearly rather than screaming like some other instructors, but he brought one cruel practice from the Peking Opera: liberal use of the stick.

The instructors held to the principle, passed down from feudal times, that "no talent grows without corporal punishment," and each carried a little stick, a symbol of authority, a constant reminder that we must practice hard and never rest. If we were caught closing our eyes or relaxing, they would hit us. We were not treated as people, and the horrible atmosphere had a lifelong negative impact on us. The fear was even worse than the physical pain and would later cause stage fright and stress in our professional lives.

The instructors had been through this themselves and did not know any better but, looking back, I wonder why they were perpetuating ancient, brutal teaching methods in a new society that was supposed to have eradicated this kind of archaic master-servant relationship. Some of the students reported the instructors' brutality to the Cultural Bureau in the hope of intervention. Cultural Bureau staff did come and make enquiries, but nothing changed: the sounds of scolding, the whistling of the cane, and the labored breathing of students who were having difficulty doing handstands were our daily symphony in the exercise hall.

In the last class of the morning, Wong taught us tumbling. Because there was only one of him and thirty of us, this exercise was more arduous for the instructor than for the students, and we finally had a slightly easier time. Still, he would use his stick on students who performed poorly and I was the worst tumbler, receiving constant reprimands.

"You are a human being!" he said. "Use your brain! Why are you so stupid? How many times have I told you what to do? How can you always forget?"

When it came to verbal abuse, Wong was actually one of the gentler ones, speaking slowly and clearly. Still, the more he scolded me, the more nervous I became, and the more errors I made. Luckily, because he had so many students to supervise, he was always too busy to punish me further.

By lunchtime, at eleven-thirty, my body felt like a dismantled machine supported by lead-filled legs. The aroma of food in the canteen would send my empty stomach into spasms. Holding the bowl and chopsticks in my hands, I would start thinking that every day was going to be like this, torture session after torture session stretching off into eternity, and the food became tasteless.

Noon till two was set aside for a nap, followed by cultural lessons. All thirty of us, equal numbers of boys and girls aged nine to fourteen, sat in a large room hung with maps, wind whistling through the cracks in the walls. I looked forward to our afternoon classes, which included Chinese, mathematics, history and geography, not because I liked those subjects but because they offered physical respite.

Dinner came at five-thirty, and from six to eight-thirty we had more lessons, which were different each night, ranging from politics to dance, music, and posture training. At nine pm, we were supposed to wash our feet and go to bed. Each and every day, except for one Sunday a month, was strictly regimented like this, with more than ten hours of training and lessons and no free time to ourselves.

At night, with my body aching all over, it was hard to fall asleep. Recalling the drills and scolding during the day, I wondered if the torture would ever stop. I still imagined forlornly that my parents might rescue me, and tears would roll down my cheeks onto the pillow. I could only cry alone in bed. After all, I was a boy, a man. A man should not shed tears in front of others, nor complain about the hardship of training drills. I would be humiliated by the other boys if I did. Most of the children in the troupe knew where their parents were, and they all seemed stronger than me. But for me, tomorrow would be a continuation of my lonely misery. And the day after tomorrow.

As if the emotional side wasn't tough enough, the heat and cold were extreme. When the temperature reached 100 degrees in summer, our exercise hall became a big steamer. Even before we made any movement, we felt dizzy and wet with sweat. Practicing handstands, I saw streams of perspiration running down my arms. On the floor, imprints of my hands were left amid dark circles of sweat.

Strangely, as time went by, the unbearable heat became bearable. But this wasn't a good feeling, more an effect of numb exhaustion. I might have lost so much bodily fluid that I went into a dream-state. During breaks in tumbling class, I observed the raised dust dancing in the shafts of sunlight slanting through the dilapidated reed roof of the exercise hall, and floated away into movie-like scenes of sunlight falling on a misty forest. The heat was only bearable because I was losing the ability to feel pain.

The cold winters were the other extreme. The bitter north-westerly wind swept through the reed roof making a loud screech. The wind cut into our bodies, which were thinly clad in our training outfits: blue cotton knickerbockers under a lightweight blue jacket, worn loose to provide freedom of movement and cinched at the waist with a belt to give our bodies shape. These clothes were good for acrobatics but terrible for winter! I felt as if my heart were frozen. My body became like an ice block, with steam coming out of my mouth. My fingers were frozen stiff like carrots, totally numb. I have no idea how we were able to perform handstands and maintain our balance.

My first winter there, in 1956, was particularly severe. Seeing us shivering in the cold and unable to do the drills one morning, Instructor Wong took two cane sticks from the wall and waved them hard, making a loud whippy noise.

"Do cartwheels as a warming-up exercise!" he yelled.

He brandished the two sticks at the students who were slow in the cartwheels. Frightened, we all tried our best so that he would not hit us. Very soon, our bodies warmed up.

"Are you still cold?" Wong asked.

"Noooo," we replied in unison.

"The winter freezes lazy people," Wong went on. That meant Wong wanted us to do more training in winter; more training did make us warmer, it was true. "As long as you exercise, you will not feel the cold. For us, in this trade, we exercise during the hottest days of summer, and the coldest days of winter, so that our bodies will become strong and be fit for all weather conditions. No matter which part of the world you find yourself performing in, you can survive and perform well."

Wong made it clear that he was talking about not only the acrobatic trade, but also a correct attitude to life.

Day after day, the drills drove each of us to the extremes of endurance. We became numb to the muscle-wrenching and skin-ripping exercises. It was cruel beyond belief, but it did its job. As we passed the initial training stage, I discovered the huge potential in the simple fact of endurance.

5

"ALL BITTERNESS WILL TURN TO SWEETNESS"

Over time, going from the exercise hall into the schoolroom after lunch began to feel like a transition from a feudalistic to a civilized society. The class teachers were kind and patient. The knowledge they taught was the wealth of human wisdom, the laws of nature and the social skills we needed to take our place in society. I came to understand the connection between humanity and the world, and also the interconnection between all things. These classes helped me feel that there was light at the end of a long tunnel.

I liked mathematics, I liked Chinese better, but I liked Teacher Su's class the best. Su read texts with passion. He wanted us to form the habit of treasuring our time, as "one inch of time on the sundial is worth one ounce of gold." His sense of urgency had a great impact on my young heart.

Su taught geography. He pointed at the map hanging on the wall and said, "You are going to be acrobats representing your country by performing abroad. If you do not even know the location of your country, your people, your history and the basic situation, how can you do your job properly?"

Go abroad and perform? What a joke. I only wished I could survive training every day!

It was in these classes that I received my initial patriotic education. I learned that I must direct my efforts toward the prosperity of China. Su said: "The map of China used to be like the shape of a mulberry leaf, but after the first Opium War, which started in 1840, China was carved up by the imperialist countries, and the mulberry has become a cockerel. This is the gravest insult, one that all Chinese must not forget."

The evening classes, such as music, dancing, self-directed study and art appreciation, were easy to cope with. Art appreciation was my favorite; it enhanced my taste, understanding and creativity. There were two components to the art appreciation class: lectures and observations. The Cultural Bureau often arranged performances by senior artists and students. We were also allowed to go to the Cultural Square, where foreign artistic groups performed in Shanghai, and saw *Swan Lake* performed by the New Siberia ballet troupe. I had not seen dancing *en pointe* before and found it amazing. The pursuit of perfection, I learned, is the motto of all successful artists.

We also listened to famous artists speak about their careers, art and lives. Gai Jiaotian, a Peking Opera performer, impressed me most. He had spent decades in the pursuit of perfection and summed up his secret in one word: "practice." After training hard each day, he would practice his own form of meditation, which he named "soul escaping the body." He would sit and relax, reflecting on what he had done in the day and, as his mind floated free, examine his physical actions. He would store the correct actions in his mind in order to practice better the next day. This kind of revision method, which I adopted, helps greatly.

Hard training and practice were rungs on the ladder to success in the higher reaches of the art, Gai said. "All bitterness will turn to sweetness, and one must taste all bitterness to become a great man." For perfect composure, for one perfect twist of his voice, he would practice over and over, taking great joy in the seemingly boring training.

Once, during a performance, Gai told us, he broke his leg when he landed badly after a high somersault. He did not leave the stage, but gritted his teeth and stood on his good leg until the curtain came down. He then fell down on the stage. An operation on his leg was unsuccessful and he was unable to perform anymore. Gai asked the doctor if there was any way that his leg could be returned to normal. The doctor said it would have to be broken again. Gai wanted to perform so much he immediately put his lame leg under the table and twisted it around the table leg to break it so that the doctor could correct the damage. Although this indeed allowed him to perform again, Gai's story shocked me. The bravery of this man! With such spirit one could become successful in whatever one chose to do. I was greatly inspired.

Gai provided a piece in the puzzle that was coming together in my head: to succeed was my destiny. Success, and fulfilling my destiny, would give purpose and direction to all I had to endure along the way. The hardship was not meaningless; on the contrary, hardship would add greater meaning to my ultimate success.

We had other visitors. To broaden our artistic views and bring some color to our lives, foreign acrobatic troupes performed for us. The first was the Soviet Union circus troupe, which came in 1956.

In the late 1920s, the Soviet government had established circus schools, which produced a lot of talent. Gymnastics, ballet, opera, music and drawing were taught along with dangerous circus acts. This led to circus performances different from any in the past. When the Soviet Union circus troupe came to Shanghai, they performed at Jiangwan Stadium, far from the inner city. We ate our dinner early and then, in great excitement, were taken to the stadium.

The performing style of the Soviet Union circus troupe was totally different from China's acrobatic troupes. A circus ring had been erected in the center of the rectangular sports stadium, with the band seated near the audience exit. Before each show, the audience was able to see the band tuning up. The show began with the song "Moscow-Beijing," well known in China due to what was then a close friendship with the Soviet Union. The audience clapped with the music; the interaction between performers and spectators created a warm atmosphere. The trapeze and animal performances, especially the tigers, caught our attention. In an iron cage, three big, fierce dogs defended the tiger trainer. Their presence added to the audience's sense of intrigue and apprehension. The tension built as the trainer, cracking his whip in one hand and holding a prod in the other, directed the tigers. Upon his instruction, the seven or eight tigers formed a line; they lay down; they rolled on the ground; they leapt; they jumped through fire rings.

These tigers were hand-raised, and had spent their lives in the cage and under the whip. They were all tame. Even though they roared when prodded and excited the audience, their roars were more a complaint than a threat.

To me, the dogs were the more interesting act. They were divided into two teams, wearing different costumes, for a game of football. When the umpire threw the ball into the air and started the game, players on both sides began to chase the ball, trying to nose it into the goal. The methods of attacking and defending were as impressive as in football played by humans. Contact was made, and dogs were barking everywhere. I did not know if they also cursed and swore like people, but certainly they did not hurt other players intentionally, as humans do.

A goalkeeping dog was held on a leash to keep it near the goal and prevent it running onto the field to join the other side. Not surprisingly, when seeing their goal was about to be penetrated, some dogs played up, chewing and tearing the ball apart. While the referee changed the ball, the defending team gained some time to organize itself. What topped the show off was when one of the goalkeepers tried to join in chasing the ball, pulling the man holding the leash off his feet and dragging him a few yards. This unexpected move ended the match.

Since we were small, we had been taught that the Soviet Union had the perfect social system for all humankind. It was with this mentality that we observed the Soviet troupe. When a French acrobatic troupe came to China a couple of years later, a rare delegation from the West, we were taken for a look. To our surprise, the French performance was also excellent. There was not a single empty space in the 10,000-seat Cultural Square and the Shanghai audience applauded, with people saying later that the French performances were in no way inferior to the Soviets'.

Because of the differences in history, culture and social systems, the French troupe had a totally different performing style. While the Soviets emphasized the unity of the whole, the French performers expressed themselves in pursuit of their own creativity and innovation. The flying trapeze act was typical of the Western style. It required the performer to execute a body spin of 540 degrees, a two and a half flip, and to end with a mid-air catch. The level of danger, the beauty of the movements, and the precision of the actions were astonishing. The quick change was another of their tricks. A female performer stood on the stage and started to turn on the spot. Whenever she completed a turn, her costume changed. After twelve turns, she had shown costumes from twelve different countries. She did so to the beat of folk music, and the color of the dresses, her tall, slim physique and the liveliness of the melody impressed me very much.

Next, two men and a woman came to the revolving stage. They were from the same place as the sculptor Rodin, and adopted sculptural poses demonstrating the harmony between humanity and nature. When they changed their positions, I felt the transformation and purification from the body to the mind, from the mundane world to the unworldly. These shows had an enormous impact on me when later I started to perform on the world stage.

*　*　*

One Sunday, Teacher Xu, the teacher in charge, asked us, "Do you want to go to the Bund Park and play?"

"Yes!" we cried.

"If yes, there is one condition. You must be tidy. No exercise dress, but you should wear a white shirt with blue trousers, and white sports shoes. And do not forget your red scarf." This was the "Young Pioneers" outfit for children in the 1950s. The little red scarf was not to be forgotten, as it symbolized uprightness and Communist progressiveness.

The monthly free Sunday was the day we longed for. We were allowed to go out for unscheduled activities and be like normal kids. For one day, we did not need to worry about being reproached by the instructors, nor about the whipping sound of the cane. The tightly knotted string was unwound a little. Each free Sunday, there would be a movie session. All of the films were in black and white and told predictably simple stories about Communist heroes.

We could also play in the troupe courtyard, and occasionally the teachers took us in a group to a park outside.

Being able to go out and play and to breathe fresh air made us all very happy. As instructed by Xu, we put on the Young Pioneers outfits and applied white chalk to our dirty sports shoes. Some boys even used white sticky tape to cover holes in the shoes. We formed a parade and got on the bus to the Bund Park, on the bank of the Huangpu River. From the park, we could see Waibaidu Bridge and buildings such as the Art Deco Peace Hotel, the Bank of China and the Shanghai Club, all landmarks of the Bund.

Under the blue sky and white clouds, I walked away from my classmates and sat quietly on the bank of the river, enjoying the breeze blowing lightly on my face. The river flowed slowly by. Cargo ships transporting lengths of timber sounded their horns. Boats covered by dark awnings swayed up the river, carrying fishermen and their families, who lived on board. A cruise ship eased in to anchor alongside the dock at Shi Liu Pu. Farther away were several big ocean liners. The yellowish water lapped at the riverbank, giving out a faint fishy smell. Across the river were huge factories and vast agricultural lands, as well as the undeveloped Pudong area.

I wondered where the river ended. Would it ever dry up? Metal sinks in water—so how come big ships built with metal could float on the water? I was reminded of the famous line Xu often quoted: "Knowledge comes from the traveling of thousands of miles, and from the reading of thousands of books."

My thoughts were interrupted by a whistle. I ran to the meeting point, where Xu told us: "The Bund Park, where you are having a great time today, used to be a foreign concession for the British and other foreign imperialist countries. At that time, a sign was put up here, saying, 'No Chinese and dogs permitted.' Class, today we are living in this beautiful city, but we must not forget the dark history it has been through. You must remember this history, so that you can understand that the good life of today did not come easily."

If the teacher said it, it had to be true.

On the Sundays when we were not allowed free time outside the compound, we often became extremely bored. One day, a classmate suggested we play hide-and-seek and I happily joined in. The next day, as soon as our exercise and training were complete, Zhao De Li, the troupe director, dismissed the girls and kept us boys behind.

"Yesterday, which one of you urinated in the rice cooker in the Pingtan troupe's kitchen?" (Pingtan is a form of ballad-singing in the Suzhou dialect, and the troupe shared the compound with us until 1960.) "The cook has complained to me. Are you out of your minds? Confess. Who urinated there?"

No one came forward. There were no suspects, so Zhao used the usual punishment: all boys were to spend twenty minutes in a hand-stand. Normally, a twenty-minute handstand was not a problem, but we were exhausted at the end of a long day's drills and exercises. Each minute was torture. But the instructors' methods worked against them this time. Torture had become a normal part of our lives, and we coped with the punishment without breaking. When I grew up, I understood that endurance is a useful characteristic. A shame that we boys learned it so early.

The following Sunday, Li Ai Di, who was the son of Teacher Li Dianqi, came over. He was the same age as me and lived in a house next door to the compound. He was a very friendly boy, and would play hide-and-seek with us on Sundays. During the week he went off to a normal school outside. I said to him: "Someone pissed in the big rice-cooking pot and all us boys in the troupe were punished."

"I did it," he said, without remorse. "The pot was left at the foot of the wall; I didn't know it was what they cooked with. I needed to go urgently, so I pissed into it."

At least that solved the mystery, and explained why none of the children in the troupe had confessed. But it didn't erase the punishment we had received!

On Sundays I liked finding a quiet place in a corner and reading picture books such as *Story of the Three Kingdoms* and *Outlaws of the Marsh*. One Sunday, when my classmates were again playing hide-and-seek, someone hid in the top awning of a truck and made the canvas dirty. The next day, the driver complained. Whenever someone found on a Monday that something had become dirty or been damaged, they accused us boys.

After dinner, a stern-faced Zhao De Li asked us, "Who started the hide-and-seek game yesterday, and dirtied the awning of the truck?"

Zhao was a fearsome sight. Around thirty years of age, he had a thick beard and a quick temper. He could put on a polite, charming face when he needed to, but when he got angry with us children he went straight for the stick. He had studied for the Peking Opera, but was unsuccessful. Before becoming the director of the school, he had been the troupe's accountant. At the time, laypeople rather than experts ran the troupe, and he knew nothing about proper methods of organizing and training. The punishments of the old society, however, he knew only too well. What annoyed him most was that we kept receiving complaints, which gave top management the impression that he was not doing a good job, and thus he lost face.

"Who started the game?" His voice was not loud but terror rose within us. This would again end in punishment. We were all looking at each other.

Qian Qinyu, an older boy who was fourteen, came forward.

"It was me."

"Come out! Lie on the long bench!"

Zhao rolled up his sleeves and, with a fierce look, started to cane

Qian. We watched in horror, not knowing how many times Zhao would hit Qian, who was clinging to the long bench. With each stroke, Qian's head came up and dropped again. We felt that the cane landed not only on Qian but on us, too. We started to shiver. One stroke, two strokes, three. Suddenly the cane snapped. The world fell silent. We looked on, horrified, at the broken cane in Zhao's hand, and at Qian, who came off the long bench and squatted in pain. His hands were on his bottom, his head tilted upwards, his face totally white. Then he grinned, showing his teeth, and beads of sweat as big as soybeans ran down his face. He did not shed a tear. His eyes shone with unyielding defiance.

What a strong man! I said to myself.

Zhao, who had thought to "kill a chicken to warn some monkeys," as the proverb has it, also looked at the broken cane, and dismissed us all. That was the end of the matter—although I spent all night puzzling over what I'd seen. Cane has a high degree of flexibility. What kind of person could hit someone so hard he would break a cane? Why did the upper management allow this kind of person to be in charge of the acrobatic school? Of course, I did not arrive at any satisfactory answers.

Sunday was also a time for cleaning and tidying up. When I was nine, I needed to learn how to wash my clothing. Looking at my three sets of dirty blue outfits, which had been accumulating during the whole week, I did not know where to start. Some girls came to my aid, showing me how to apply the soap, how to rub and how to rinse, and then helped hang my clothes on the lines. Sometimes one of them, Zhou Yanji, would even wash my clothing for me. Those girls, only twelve or thirteen themselves, often helped me with stitching up the holes and tears in my bed sheets, and mending my clothing and socks. They even helped me wash around my neck. This care felt like the love of family; I have never forgotten it. It was one of the rare experiences of tenderness that I had. Through their kindness, I came to realize that I too should help others.

Time is an amazing thing. Mostly people only feel the change from day to night, the coming of spring and the going of winter. For us children, the passing of time changed everything, including the way we experienced suffering.

When I was ten, one night I was lying in bed when I heard a song being played. It was "Awaara Hoon," from the Indian movie *Awaara*. The lyrics went:

> I am but alone
> I am the destitute
> The world to me is like a desert
> With no signs of life around
> I am in no contact with anyone
> I am like a star lost in the dark night
> Roaming around
> My destiny is so unfortunate
> But I am not feeling sad
> I don't feel sad at all
> I hide my bitterness in my heart
> And sing happily
> Who can stop me from singing?
> Oh, destiny, my destiny, my star
> Please answer me
> Why are you torturing me so relentlessly?

That night, a year after I arrived at the compound, I was surprised to find that I could listen to the song without feeling pain or bitterness. I felt I had grown up, and I thanked time for lifting the shadow from my heart.

6

MY STAGE DEBUT

In 1957, our troupe was looking for a top talent for one of its teeterboard shows. The teeterboard is like a seesaw: an oak plank about 3 yards in length, propped on a fulcrum in the middle. One performer stands on the low end of the plank and another performer jumps from a high point, often after bouncing on a trampoline, onto the upper end, which propels the first performer into a trick like a somersault.

The instructors chose me—I didn't know why, I just did what I was told—and I was sent on the road to perform with the troupe. We traveled to Shandong, Beijing and other places. In the mornings I worked on my teeterboard skills, and in the evenings I appeared in a magic show where I had to emerge from a box. At ten years old, I was a stage performer.

That year, there was a nationwide epidemic of flu. I fell victim a few days after we arrived in Qingdao, a major city in Shandong Province in the north of China near Beijing. But the show must go on, and I had to perform even with a high temperature. For the magic show, I had to crawl through a hidden partition into the box, which was being turned on stage. But on this occasion, as I waited behind the partition, stricken with fever, I fell asleep. When a gun-shot was fired, announcing the opening of the box, I was shocked awake. The box opened; the whole audience saw me in a panic, try-ing to crawl from the partition into the box, and burst out laughing. Well, I was living proof that on-the-job training was not viable in a performing group, and I was sent back to the acrobatic school for more coaching.

By 1958, the Great Leap Forward movement was at its peak. The Chinese government had declared that our industrial and agri-cultural sectors could not progress at "walking pace," but needed to increase their output at an extreme rate. The standard routines at the troupe were not in harmony with this directive, and manage-ment was required to produce some new plan to revolutionize our training for our own great leap forward. The troupe was preparing to perform at the International Children's Festival, and producing a revolutionary advance in time for this performance would greatly disturb the existing five-year training plan. But orders were orders, and the whole troupe started a program that was so hard we had to practice day and night. The managers wanted to impress the Cul-tural Bureau, teachers wanted their pupils to shine on stage, and some of the older students saw an opportunity to kickstart their artistic careers.

On the big day, parents took their children and teachers took their students to a big circus tent. As an eleven-year-old performing officially for the first time, I was battling nerves. I was afraid of doing poorly and then being reproached by the teachers. I was worried about falling and injuring myself. I was scared the audience would laugh at me. The two performances I took part in were the flying trapeze net and the highwire, both of which frightened me. I would be performing a handstand on top of the head of another performer, who was balancing on a highwire! Waiting to go on stage, I had

Shanghai, 1958: My nerve-wracking first official appearance on stage. I am performing the handstand.

Shanghai, 1959: I am practicing launching a tumble for the trio teeterboard.

butterflies in my stomach. My palms were sweaty and I could not wipe them dry.

When it was my turn to perform, I acquitted myself well. But there were complex feelings inside me, not just nerves. Looking out and seeing children with their parents, I couldn't hold back a wave of loneliness. I told myself to be proud—I was starting my artistic career at age eleven—but those positive thoughts were battling with my sadness and fear.

After these performances, the troupe went into half-training, half-performing mode.

In the spring of 1959, at the Chinese Communist Party's national conference in Shanghai, we performed for the public, as well as for the CCP members. One night, halfway through our program, an order came from the Cultural Bureau that we were to go and join another group to give two extra performances: the trio teeterboard and a very difficult traditional magic trick that involved producing various items, such as a burning stick and a fish in a saucepan full of water. From the depths of a changshan, a slim-fitting Chinese dress. The bureau said we did not need to change clothes and provided vehicles to take us. As to the location and audience, we were not informed.

We climbed into a car and were driven along Yan'an Road to the west. We turned right into Maoming Road, which had no pedestrians and seemed strangely quiet. There were only a few couples about, whom we were later told were police officers in disguise. At eight pm our car stopped in front of the Jin Jiang Club, right opposite the Jin Jiang Hotel. Formerly the French Club, it had a top-class dance floor. In the new China, the club was for officials only. That night, high officials of the Central Committee of the Communist Party were there for a ball. We were to perform during the breaks.

The ball had already started. At one end of the dance hall were three bands. One consisted of Western string instruments, one consisted of wind instruments and the last was a Chinese folk music band. We waited at the side, near the bands. There were three-seat sofas on both sides of the dance floor. Premier Zhou Enlai and Foreign Minister Chen Yi were sitting on one of these, while on small round tables, green tea and Panda cigarettes were served. The leaders danced and chatted, and the mood was relaxed.

Zhu De, the co-founder and commander-in-chief of the Red Army, arrived soon afterwards. Not long after he sat down, he was invited onto the floor by one of several women whose specific task was to dance with the leaders. In contrast to Premier Zhou's elegant dancing, Zhu maintained a military rigidity. After a few dances, he left. Then the music came to an abrupt halt and all the lights in the hall came on. Chairman Mao Zedong walked in, greeted the leaders present, and sat down on the three-seat couch on the west side of the dance floor. We were only a few steps away from him. Once the chairman was seated, staff went up to offer tea and cigarettes. Several prearranged dance partners also lined up, ready.

The music resumed, and the lights were dimmed again. I felt the atmosphere had become heavier with Chairman Mao's arrival. All the officials left a space around him, and nobody dared go near his couch. For a while he listened to the music, tapping his hand on the seat back—not keeping very good time, I noticed. When he got up and selected a woman for a dance, the other dancers on the floor squeezed closer together, trying to leave more room for the chairman who, right hand tapping on his partner's back to the music, glided with light steps to well-known songs such as "Liuyang River," "Nanniwan" and "Zi Zhu Diao." As soon as each new piece started, all of the dance partners competed to dance with Mao. I noticed a young woman sitting to one side. She did not get one dance with

Mao and became very saddened. I could see how much the chairman meant to these people.

After performing the traditional Chinese magic trick, we were scheduled for the trio teeterboard. I wanted it to be over, so I could relax. To my disappointment, an opera, *You Long Xi Feng* (*The Wandering Dragon Toys with the Phoenix*), was inserted ahead of our performance. It's a story about Emperor Zhengde, who, when traveling in plain clothes to the town of Meilong, has a flirtation with a local woman, Sister Phoenix.

The show starred Tong Zhiling, a famous Peking Opera performer. She looked amazing to me. Although, as a boy of twelve, I did not understand the subtle mystery of a dragon playing with a phoenix, I could tell by Chairman Mao's close attention and appreciative smile that the show must have been very interesting.

It was midnight when our act began. Extremely tired, we became more nervous. When performing, one of the girls made a mistake. She should have turned her body, but instead she slipped upside down. The person who was supposed to catch her did not react swiftly enough, so she fell to the ground, landing on her head, and lay there with no sign of life. Panic struck the whole hall. At the moment of the accident, I looked at Mao Zedong. He sat calmly as if nothing had happened.

The girl was sent to hospital by ambulance, but was discharged the next day. She hadn't hurt herself when she fell; she was just too shocked to move. We had gone into that night's performance with high expectations, but we left the scene in haste, with heavy hearts.

Shanghai, 1959: The infamous trio teeterboard stunt.

7

THE GREAT WORLD

The foreign minister of the People's Republic looked me in the eye. My stomach fluttered with nerves.

"My little friends," he said, "not only should you practice and master your acrobatic skills, you must also have international knowledge, so that you can complete the task your country has bestowed on you."

The entire troupe was gathered, attired in unfamiliar Western-style clothes, in the Hall of Purple Light in Zhongnanhai, the heart of China's politics. Our host was Foreign Minister Chen Yi, who, like Premier Zhou Enlai, was highly respected in artistic circles. Because he had been the mayor of Shanghai for nine years, we felt a special affinity with Chen Yi. He was wearing a brown corduroy dress suit and a pair of cloth shoes. Sitting right in front of us, he spoke as if having a casual chat with friends. But this was an important briefing for our international mission.

He said the Chinese government strongly supported the independence movements in Asia, Africa and Latin America, and strongly opposed the new colonization policies of imperialist countries. He told us our performances in Africa would enhance China's influence there, delivering a message to Africans that our country supported them. All countries, he said, irrespective of size and wealth, were equal. When others came to our country, we, as a host, would accommodate our guests. When we went to another country, we needed to respect the people, be courteous, and not display any chauvinism.

Then he asked: "Do you know who Kishi Nobusuke is?"

We had no idea, and looked at each other without answering.

He went on: "Kishi Nobusuke is the Japanese prime minister. But do you know if he is a good person or a bad person?"

"Bad person. Japan is one of the countries that invaded China. Their prime minister must be a bad person," we young ones replied.

"Correct. He is a bad person. Good answer." The atmosphere in the hall became more relaxed. Then Chen Yi asked the adults: "Do you know who Fu Cong is?"

"Yes," someone replied. "He is China's best pianist. He even studied in Poland. He defected in 1958 while attending an international music competition."

"Correct. But after he ran away, he did not speak ill of the Chinese Communist Party. He only said that the hands used to play the piano should not be used to hold a hoe."

This was a surprisingly liberal comment, and we left the one-hour reception with a favorable impression of Chen Yi.

The pre-trip political briefings went from November 1959 to January 1960. Government checks, required for those few people allowed to travel overseas, were in two parts, political and professional. The former, conducted in Shanghai by the troupe's own personnel department and the local police, the Shanghai Public Security Bureau, scrutinize our political behavior, speech and, of course the most important one, loyalty to the ruling party and its leader. I knew what to say, and followed the script.

The professional part was conducted in Beijing, where our per-formance was examined by the Chinese People's Association for Friendship with Foreign Countries, or Friendship Association. One night while we were performing, Premier Zhou Enlai came in. He had a kind face and sat with a respectful, amiable half-smile. His arrival made us realize how much importance the central govern-ment attached to this trip.

In order to impress Premier Zhou, leaders of the troupe wanted to perform on the aerial rings, and this led to complaints from the audience, who had already seen these tricks. After learning this, the premier sent his secretary backstage to ask that the show not be altered by his presence. We were impressed by his humility.

Like anyone going abroad, we had to complete a course in political studies. The director of the trip, Qu Wu from the Friend-ship Association, gave speeches outlining the excellence of the sit-uation in China, as well as the economy, geography, peoples, history and current political situation in the countries we would visit. The Friendship Association also arranged a visit to the Bei-jing Red Star Commune, built to celebrate the tenth anniversary of the new China. It was exciting to see this perfect farming village, and it reinforced everything we had heard about the prosperity of our great country.

Because of a recent air tragedy in East Germany, and also because a member of an artistic troupe had been assassinated in North Vietnam, the leaders instructed us to be on high alert, and to abide strictly by foreign affairs rules. We had receptions and checks, studies and inoculations for which we had to fill out our "yellow books." With all this happening, we thought our departure could be at any time. But we were delayed for weeks. We stayed at the Dongsi Hotel to continue our studies, and practiced our drills at the China Acrobatic Troupe headquarters in Bei Xin Qiao. The dry climate in

Beijing brought down many troupe members with colds, and the immunizations caused some adverse reactions. The troupe doctors were kept very busy looking after everyone. On top of that, the frequent blackouts due to insufficient power did not make life easy. A sense of foreboding grew; were we ever going to go, or was something happening behind the scenes that might keep us in this holding pattern indefinitely?

To calm us down, leaders from the Friendship Association came to explain.

"We are waiting for visas for all the countries that we are going to visit. Apart from the Soviet Union and some other socialist countries in Eastern Europe, we have diplomatic relations with only a few countries. We need to visit many countries on this trip, and some are refusing to give us visas on the grounds that we have not established diplomatic relationships with them. Dear comrades, please be assured, all relevant parties are trying their best to negotiate. Once the visa issue is cleared up, we will depart immediately."

Foreign diplomats joked that China's diplomatic relations were with small friends, poor friends, and female friends who were the wives of the small and poor presidents.

At last, the day came. On January 8, 1960, after more than one month's intensive training in Beijing, the Shanghai Acrobatic Troupe took off on a tour of Africa. Our group consisted of about fifty performers and staff, among them a Baghdad-based text journalist from the Xinhua News Agency, a Cairo-based photographic journalist, two video photographers from China Central Television, one doctor and four interpreters, three of whom spoke English and one French. The flight took the northern route, from Beijing to Africa via Moscow. Before the split between China and the Soviet Union, most Chinese delegations took this route.

Filled with curiosity and wearing a Western suit, I waited to board the Soviet-made propeller-driven China Airlines Ilyushin Il-18. Some of the adults in the troupe had high expectations, but I was just going along with the crowd. I was eager to see people and nations with different histories, situations and social structures.

Before boarding, everyone carrying a fountain pen was asked to squeeze all the ink out because the pressurized cabin might cause the ink to explode over our shirts. A lot of us went to the toilet to do this. Once we had boarded, air hostesses brought out a tray of fruit candies, the usual practice in those years, to help avoid air pressure causing discomfort in our ears.

When the plane took off, accelerating through the clouds into the blue sky, the speed threw me back against my seat. Soon we were basking in glorious golden sunlight. It felt like it was always tranquil yet brilliant up there. No wonder all the deities in the old legends chose the sky as their abode.

After landing in snow-clad, minus 22-degree Irkutsk, Siberia, we changed to a Tu-104 and flew to Omsk to refuel before continuing to Moscow. I was "traveling a thousand miles," as Teacher Xu had said, to check out the geography of the world, where the five great continents and four big oceans meet. The politics teacher had told us that two-thirds of the people in the world were yet to be emancipated. That was the beginning and end of my knowledge. For a child of my age, it was too early to want to pay attention to politics, and yet I was living in China, where everything was politically saturated. A child's mind is like a piece of blotting paper: it will absorb whichever color is applied to it. I had no choice but to take in what I was told.

By the time we descended into Moscow, it was pitch black outside with thick clouds close to the ground, making landing very difficult, even dangerous. The plane tried three times before it could land safely. The two failed attempts horrified the older ones in our group, and everyone had their faces pressed against the windows. Twice there were cries of "It failed again!" I was so engrossed in the new experience that I did not recognize the danger we were in.

We stayed at the Hotel Ukraina on the Moskva River. After the long multi-leg flight, and with a five-hour time difference, everyone was exhausted. I had no strength to appreciate the hotel's luxuries. I had a bath using the towel as my washcloth, amazed that foreigners would use such a big towel to wash themselves. Small cloths should have been enough! After the bath, I fell onto the soft mattress, and as soon as my head hit the pillow, I was sound asleep.

* * *

The next morning, before sunrise, we were awakened by a familiar song from our childhood, "Wide is My Motherland," ringing from a bell tower in the Kremlin.

O, my homeland is a spacious country:
Streams and fields and forests full and fair.
I don't know of any other country
Where a man can breathe a freer air!

I opened the thick curtain and looked down at the snow-covered, sleeping city. I felt wonderful, as if in a peaceful fairytale world.

I went to the restaurant for breakfast, which included black caviar, but was puzzled by the sequence in which the dishes arrived and which cutlery to use. To avoid drawing attention to myself, I focused so hard on copying what the others were eating, and how they were eating it, that I did not enjoy my breakfast.

I was surprised to find, on the snow-white tablecloth, some

delicate plates piled high with dark bread. When I was in the orphanage, we ate dark buns mixed with bran. I remembered an article in one of our textbooks about life in the Soviet Union soon after the October Revolution. The imperialist countries had imposed an economic embargo, and everything was in scarce supply. Lenin, leader of the revolution, also ate dark bread mixed with bran. A play, "Lenin Eating Dark Bread," was even performed by the older orphans to show that Lenin lived just like us.

I asked an older member of our troupe sitting next to me, who had been to Eastern Europe previously, "Why do grand hotels such as the Ukraina serve dark bread?"

"It is nutritious, good for the digestion and delicious when spread with black caviar accompanied by ham and egg."

I wondered what food Lenin had eaten with his dark bread.

Since I was little, I had been taught that there were two famous squares in the world: Tiananmen Square, where Chairman Mao had proclaimed the independence of the new China; and Red Square in Moscow, where the tombs of Lenin and Stalin could be seen. On that day, the snow was like the pure white down of a goose. The cold wind whipped the long queue waiting solemnly to visit the tombs. Due to a special arrangement by our tour guide, we were escorted to the front of the queue. No one voiced any complaint. They just kept waiting. The powerful, almost religious, sincerity of the people was very impressive, adding to the somber charm of Red Square.

Guards stood motionless around the tombs, ignoring the cold wind and the snowflakes. Were it not for the vapor coming from their mouths, I might have thought they were statues. Their stillness added to the mystic atmosphere.

My heart filled with awe. Holding my breath, I walked timidly through the door in the Kremlin wall. I tried not to make a sound. I stared at the crystal coffins in which Lenin and Stalin were laid.

Lenin's body was placed in his coffin in 1924, while Stalin had died in 1953. With the passing of time, Lenin's face had changed color slightly. Stalin, however, in his military uniform, looked as if he had gone to sleep only the night before.

After that, we went to visit Moscow University on Lenin Hills. The grandeur of the academic buildings showed how much importance the government attached to this university. The Soviet Union was a huge magnet, attracting young students from Asia, Africa and Latin America. The subway system in Moscow was like a spiderweb covering the whole city, its stations decorated with marble sculptures. Huge crowds came and went, but everything looked to be in fine order. The people dressed elegantly and showed great courtesy, with peaceful faces. To us this demonstrated the underlying greatness of Russian culture.

We left Moscow for Cairo on another Tu-104. Due to bad weather, we had to change course and go via Budapest in Hungary for a one-day stopover. We stood on the bank of the Danube, with dark clouds hanging above, watching the river flowing between Buda and Pest. The cold westerly wind raised pale gray ripples on the river, sending chills through my body and depressing my mood. I cheered myself with the thought that in spring, the scenery must be different. A boat trip on the River Danube in the sun would be much nicer than this bleak scene.

Hungary was the most open of the socialist Eastern European countries, with a sound economy. Budapest was a modern city and we could see the strong economic power in the people's clothing, the commodities available in the shops and the crowded market. The one eyesore was the Swiss cheese-like pattern of bullet holes in many of the buildings, a reminder of the Soviet army's suppression of Hungary in 1956. Some members of our troupe had been witnesses to the Hungarian Revolution. I wanted a first-hand story of the historic event, but was disappointed. They would not tell us about it.

When we landed in Cairo, the weather was beautiful. The boulevards from the airport to the city were dotted with palm trees, as well as hedge-like trees that had been trimmed into barrels and prisms. We saw a tall building with a mosque adjacent to it, luxury cars sharing the road with donkeys, and hawkers on bicycles with breadbaskets on their heads, crisscrossing the main streets and the small lanes.

Cairo, 1960: A naive me, aged thirteen, on the banks of the Nile during the tour of Africa.

The magnificent pyramids filled us with amazement. Standing in front of these seemingly impossible structures built by human hands, I wondered how the people of several thousand years ago could have stacked up all those huge stones.

Not far from one of the pyramids, the tour guide pointed at a pit and told us a boat had been unearthed there. It was a burial object, on which the pharaohs could cruise the Nile after their death. The pharaohs, who had exhausted their nation's treasure in the building of their tombs, were pursuing eternity in two worlds, both alive

Cairo, 1960: From the Great Wall to the Pyramids, I had seen two of the Seven Wonders of the World. Here I am in the front right.

and dead. But the pyramids had become a major attraction, with millions of tourists disturbing the pharaohs' rest. Perhaps not what King Khufu intended!

As we traveled south to Sudan, our troupe was divided into two in case of terrorism or mechanical aircraft failure. If our plane went down, the government didn't want to lose the entire troupe. I was too young to worry about safety, and did not care which group I traveled in, as long as the flight was not too bumpy or too painful for my eardrums. I became good friends with one of the girls in our traveling group, Zhou Yanji, who had helped look after me back in Shanghai. She was an excellent foot juggler who eventually performed for Mao Zedong. Four years older than me, she was a quiet person, less interested in talking to me than in observing Africa, and she kept a diary which would, many years later, bring much of that trip back to life for me.

We flew into Sudan, a poor country with rich resources. In Khartoum, nicknamed the "furnace of the world," we could not find a decent hotel so we moved into an old yacht moored on the Nile. At a time when air-conditioners were not standard, we enjoyed the sunset on the river and the cool evening breeze—much better than hot hotel rooms! We were also able to fish, but sadly could not swim because there were crocodiles in the river.

The Sudanese people welcomed our performances, but we worked in shabby premises. The only decent place for us to perform was the open-air theater in Khartoum. Elsewhere, performances took place on makeshift stages in windy and dusty squares. The Sudanese government arranged for us to perform only in the north of the country. We requested permission to perform in the south but it was rejected on the grounds of safety. It was no secret that there was conflict between the north and the south, so we did not press our request.

Our accommodation and food, away from Khartoum, were on a chartered train. With no promotion apart from posters and newspaper commentaries, we were able to attract audiences by word of mouth. The number of shows increased due to popular demand, and tickets became hard to get. For our last performance in Sudan, back in Khartoum, the audience packed the passageways and the theater manager said, "This theater has never before encountered such a magnificent scene."

Like many other performers, I would look at the audience from the wings to see how popular we were. When we were in Sudan's second-biggest city, I peeked from behind the curtain to see how many people were in the audience and was surprised to see that the spectators, whether old or young, whether they were lovers or not, or a family, sat in separate male and female areas. That was the first and last time I saw something like this.

One of the prominent families in Sudan was descended from Muhammad Ahmad, Sudan's great Islamic religious leader. The head of the family invited us to cruise the Nile on his yacht. The yacht sailed slowly past the place where the White Nile and the Blue Nile meet. In the background were oases and ancient mosques, camels walking slowly along the riverbank, men in white robes and women with black veils waving to us.

All of this made the trip so much more memorable, and our successful performances in Sudan laid good groundwork for our future shows in Africa. At the request of the Sudanese government, we put on a special performance for the president, Ibrahim Abboud. When we came back to Sudan a few days later, after performing in Ethiopia, Chinese embassy staff told us that the United States had decided to dispatch its ice-ballet troupe to perform there, to offset the political and cultural influence of the Shanghai Acrobatic Troupe.

Khartoum, 1960: The night of our performance for the president of Sudan, Ibrahim Abboud (center). I am second from the right in the front row, and to my left is Ambassador Wang Yutian. First on the left is trip director Qu Wu.

Ethiopia was the second stop on our tour of Africa. Under the rule of Haile Selassie I, this former colonial country that had suffered strife and war was now at peace. Ethiopia was the only one of the four countries on our list that did not have a diplomatic relationship with China, and the only one represented at the United Nations. In the Korean War, Chinese forces had engaged with Ethiopian soldiers, who caused China great losses in the Battle of Triangle Hill. This had been a considerable stumbling block in the establishment of diplomatic relations, but to strengthen them, Wang Yutian, China's new ambassador to Sudan, traveled with our troupe, which created extra stress and work for us.

Ethiopia was considered a wealthy country in East Africa, and the cottage hotels we stayed in were quite comfortable. American air force staff and their families were long-term residents and whenever we met, we bade them good morning, even though we were being cautious.

Ethiopia, known as the "roof of Africa," has an average altitude of more than twelve hundred feet. This created difficulties for us because of the lack of oxygen in the air. The Soviet Union embassy instructed their hospital to bring oxygen supplies and nurses to the Haile Selassie Theater to assist the troupe doctor. The Soviet hospital was a product of the excellent long-term relationship between Russia and Ethiopia since before the October Revolution. We were told that a little boy had been brought from the royal palace in Ethiopia to Russia, and later he became the great poet Pushkin. Whether or not this was true, I was overjoyed to learn it in Ethiopia. One of his poems, the unforgettable "Monument," came to mind:

News of me will spread throughout great Russia.
And my name will be spoken in every language there.

On February 24, Emperor Haile Selassie and his wife, Empress Menen Asfaw, came to the theater named in his honor and sat in the medieval European-style royal box with red curtains to watch us perform. One of our newer acts was to walk on inflated balls while progressing over the teeterboard, two or three of us at a time, which impressed the audience greatly. During the interval, the stern-looking emperor, with the empress by his side, received Ambassador Wang Yutian and the whole troupe. He personally handed a gold coin to each of us as a souvenir.

Addis Ababa, 1960: We performed this trick of walking on inflated balls throughout our Africa trip, which included Ethiopia and Guinea. Here I am second in the line on the ball.

In April, we bade farewell to the cool of Ethiopia to return to 115-degree heat in Khartoum. Our sweat evaporated so fast that our bodies were covered in salt. We spent two weeks resting in the Chinese embassy's residence, doing training drills and studying, before flying to Guinea. It was evening when I boarded a propeller plane, run by a small airline, with part of the troupe to fly west across the African continent. As the plane was about to lift off the runway, there was a sudden engine failure, and also a problem with the propellers. The plane stopped and the passengers were required to disembark. Many of us had taken travel sickness medication beforehand and were sleeping. When we were awakened by the air hostess, and seeing that the plane was on land, we thought we had arrived in Guinea! More than ten hours later, we boarded the plane again with an uneasy feeling in our hearts. An adult troupe member sitting next to me kept mumbling, "Damn you, propeller. Don't you fail in midair."

The other half of the troupe had arrived in Guinea well before us. They had experienced strong turbulence, we heard later, and their plane descended quickly, the cabin filling with screams of terror. Our group behaved better when we encountered turbulence, but someone was yelling, "Doomed! Doomed! This time we are really doomed!"

Fortunately, the propeller worked, which was a great relief, but the turbulence kept pushing the plane up and down. I started to feel sick and this was made worse by the disgusting smell of the cigarette which the young performer sitting next to me was puffing on. I have hated smoking ever since. Eventually we landed safely in Conakry, Guinea's capital. From then on, the troupe used "been to death and back" as our synonym for flying.

Guinea, an independent country since 1958, was a sad sight. Apart from a shabby cinema in Conakry, we had to do our shows in open squares in the other nine cities, with timber floorboards, borrowed from the Guinea National Theater, placed on oil drums to create makeshift stages.

The weather in Guinea was very unpredictable. We had to perform in the scorching sun, in the wind and dust, and also in heavy rain. We traveled in a bus made in Czechoslovakia, with sealed windows but no air-conditioning, designed for the European climate. Traveling in the tropical heat near the equator for about twelve hundred miles on winding mountain roads was a real test for all of us. We called it the steam-room bus, and all jokingly called ourselves "General Heat-Enduring." I was grateful for the training I had had in the really hot summers in Shanghai.

In one city, there was not even a hotel, so the male acrobats had to sleep in the bus while the women rented two rooms and slept on rugs on the floor. Without any quilts or blankets, we had to cover ourselves with raincoats. We carried on in determined silence. What others could endure I could also endure.

China had attached great importance to the establishment of diplomatic relations with Guinea, and Liu Shaoqi, who had by then taken over as chairman of the People's Republic of China, had entrusted our trip director, Qu Wu, with a very precious jade carving to give to the president, Sékou Touré. We invited President Touré and his wife to the shabby theater to watch our premiere show, after which they, accompanied by Ke Hua, China's ambassador, joined us on the stage. The following day, Ambassador Ke Hua was very happy, telling us that the performance had greatly helped the embassy's work.

While in Conakry, we were driven in embassy vehicles to the beach. Swimming in the Atlantic Ocean was a novelty. I had learned to swim in public pools in Shanghai, but had never swum in nature: nobody would consider going into the filthy Huangpu River. Here the water was warm and fresh-smelling, the surface smooth as silk. Sitting on the soft white sand, looking at the horizon above the blue sea, I wondered what my classmates in Shanghai were doing. I might have been seeing the world, one of a privileged few, but I was so conditioned to a life of relentless practice, drills and performances that my attitude to each day was one of simple endurance.

Conakry, 1960: In the front row, President Touré is fourth from the left, and Ke Hua is third from the right. I am second on the right, beside him.

Guinea, 1960: The troupe and I visited rural areas. I am at the front left of this group.

For clothing, the women in Guinea wrapped a piece of cloth around their bodies. Married women covered their breasts, while the unmarried young women wrapped the cloth around their waist, baring their breasts. For someone like me, just entering puberty, this was quite a sight!

While performing in Guinea, we had the opportunity to watch people dancing around bonfires to the beat of drums, pounding their feet, genuinely expressing their feelings. These dances did not have any story or man-made meanings; they were a form of pure emotional expression. We also saw some shows in Guinea. In one, topless young girls lined up and stomped their feet to the strong beat of the drums. Their breasts shook violently, in a powerful display of youthful exuberance. There were arrangements between the Shanghai Acrobatic Troupe and the Guinean national song and dance troupe to exchange visits, but if this show were to be performed in China, it would clash seriously with Chinese ideology, tradition and customs! Qu Wu, our director, told the Guinean officials as much. Four years later, I was in Shanghai watching the Guinean song and dance troupe; the female performers wore an extra piece of cloth, covering their breasts.

From Guinea we flew north to Morocco. On the plane, I looked west at the sun setting above the golden Sahara. The endless sea of sand looked amazing, capturing my interest more than anything else in Africa. There I was, high up in the sky in a small plane looking down on a great desert, and I felt that sudden shock that comes when one feels so small in the vastness of nature.

Morocco was a beautiful country, with a perfect road network for smooth traveling to all the cities. Considerably different from the other former French colonies we had visited, Morocco was on the path to modernity while keeping its strong Arabic culture and traditions. We were shown around cities and their old towns. In the labyrinth of small lanes and in the crowded, bustling markets, we saw Berber women in veils and men in long robes.

A lot of habits can be changed in a new environment, but our food tastes were an exception. We quickly became tired of African food, and had prepared by packing soy sauce cubes and pickled turnips from Yunnan Province. We were very happy to find some Chinese restaurants run by Vietnamese Chinese in Morocco.

In the garden of the royal palace in Rabat, we performed for King Mohammed V. The palace gardens reminded us of scenes from the movie *The Thief of Baghdad,* with well-pruned trees, colorful flowers and buildings decorated with blue mosaics. Imperial guards patrolled the garden, holding their ancient weapons, and maids tiptoed in and out. I felt as if I were living in the middle of one of the tales from *The Thousand and One Nights.*

King Mohammed V reclined on a long couch with the queen and his concubines, who were unveiled for the occasion. We were instructed not to look at the unveiled women, and the band was placed facing away from them. Driven by curiosity, we discreetly scanned the audience. It was a stunning scene: the king lazed on the couch, surrounded by concubines with big noses and big eyes, white skin and dark hair, and beautiful figures. The seventy-two concubines in China's imperial courts were only in novels. What I saw here was a living royal court.

After the show, the royal palace expressed a wish to pay us. Director Qu Wu replied: "We have come here for friendship, not for money. It has been an honor to perform in front of the king." Then we were treated to a meal of couscous pilaf, which we ate with our hands while sitting on the floor.

As in the other African countries, our Moroccan shows were a tremendous success. With favorable reviews and an increased number of shows, our reputation grew. In one of the smaller Moroccan towns, a lot of people were not able to get in to see the show after the main gate had been shut. Police were mobilized to prevent them from entering, but the cordon was broken and a large group rushed into the performance area. We were in a walled enclosure, and when those people rushed in, it looked as if the whole town had come! Even though they had gatecrashed and had no tickets, we gave them our best performance, as usual.

Casablanca, or "white house" in Spanish, was the biggest city in Morocco, made famous by its namesake film. During the afternoon on the day of our first performance in Casablanca, a Moroccan girl came to our hotel and started to talk to us with the assistance of an interpreter. The interpreter asked a couple of us younger perform- ers to join the conversation to make it more interesting. The girl was very pretty. Her eyes were big with long eyelashes, and she stood about five feet, four inches tall.

"How old are you?" we asked.

When she said "fourteen," no one believed her. She seemed twenty years older. She was very open and talkative, perhaps because of the Western-style education she had received. She liked China and Chinese culture. She always paid attention to the rare Chinese crafts that appeared in the Moroccan market, especially those with Chinese writing on them. She also liked Chinese food, often went to Chinese restaurants and even tried to cook Chinese at home. There were not many Chinese people in Morocco, which was why she had come to our hotel. Once, she said, she had seen two Chinese people talking in the street. Even though she didn't know what they were talking about, she listened to them and watched them. She liked the expressions on their faces when they talked, and also their tones.

"The biggest wish in my life," she announced, "is to marry a Chinese man!"

We gave her a movie magazine in Chinese. We didn't expect to see her again, but on the second day she returned and showed us two pages of handwritten Chinese, a description of the movie *Zhu Fu* (*New Year Sacrifice*), which she had spent several hours copying the night before. "It was difficult at the beginning," she said, "but I kept on with it, and am very proud of my effort." I felt embarrassed, as I had never done a copying job as good as she had done!

We nicknamed her "China-Fancy" because she was so mad about things Chinese. For the few days we were in Casablanca, she came to meet with us in our hotel or the theater. What impressed me most in Morocco was not the cities or the sights, but "China-Fancy," this girl who liked China so much.

8

WEST TO EAST

We departed Africa from Tangier, a port on the Strait of Gibraltar, taking a plane to London, where it was either raining or cloudy. The sun came out for brief spells before hiding behind the clouds again, like a shy little girl. Not long before, we had been worrying about the scorching sun in Africa! Here, huge buildings were half hidden in the smog, a scene that reminded me of the London of *Oliver Twist*.

It was interesting to be in the center of "the empire on which the sun never sets." We went to the home of imperialism itself, Buckingham Palace, but as a child I was more impressed by the grand building and the beautiful uniforms of the guards than critiquing capitalism. We visited the British Museum, which I knew of not because of their unique collections, but for Karl Marx, who had spent years there working on his book *Das Kapital*. This, in the middle of the capitalist world, was the foundation of the Communism under which we lived. We stood with awe and respect at the seat in the reading room where Marx had sat. We had been told in China that the carpet had become so worn one could see the imprint of his two shoes. He, like us, knew discipline and endurance.

It was hard to imagine Marx sitting in a seat no different from any other seat there, writing a book which it seemed could only be understood by heavenly beings. I could not see the legendary pair of footmarks. We went to the Chinese section of the museum and saw paintings, calligraphy, porcelain, jade, and Chinese imperial seals, even a fresco from Dunhuang. Every piece of the collection seemed to be telling us how, since the first Opium War in 1840, the Western imperial powers had been robbing China of its treasures.

One of us asked a member of staff why the museum had such a large collection of Chinese art. He replied lightly that British people were very interested in oriental art. The theft of treasures from a weaker country was simply explained away as an interest! So this was the so-called civilized world, where the strong prey on the weak. What I could not know then was that Mao Zedong's looming Cultural Revolution would destroy vast quantities of Chinese art. At least the colonial thieves had kept their oriental treasures safe and in good order. These matters were never as simple as our ideological masters would have had us believe, but as I stood in the British Museum, I was a firm thirteen-year-old patriot.

The next day, we bought fresh flowers and went to Highgate Cemetery in the north of London to see Marx's grave. I felt extremely privileged to have this opportunity. The great pity was that red paint had been smeared on the head of the sculpture of Marx, so we could not take a photograph.

The Chinese Liaison Office was in the same old house where the Qing dynasty embassy once was. In 1896, Dr. Sun Yat-sen, the leader of the popular revolution that brought down the Qing dynasty in 1911, was kidnapped in London by the embassy staff and detained on the top floor, awaiting deportation to China where he was to be executed. Luckily, the kidnapping was made public and led to an international incident. Dr. Sun was released and became famous.

Accompanied by the embassy staff, we visited the attic where he had been detained. Seeing that normal little room brought home the individual human scale of some of the great twists of history.

Before we left Britain, the Chinese Liaison Office decided ad hoc that we should give a performance. It fell on a weekend, making it difficult to rent a theater and retrieve our costumes from the docks. However, if you have money, anything can be arranged, and the Liaison Office took care of everything. China had few other diplomatic relationships with western European countries, so the purpose of this show was obvious. We quickly shed our relaxed mood, and went into the usual nervous pre-show routines.

The show was, once again, very successful. The famous African-American singer Paul Robeson and his wife came on stage to congratulate us, along with Chinese officials from the Liaison Office. Robeson was one of the few pro-China Americans known to us. As early as spring 1941, he issued a Chinese album, *Chee Lai: Songs of New China,* including a song which later became our national anthem. After being blacklisted during the anti-Communist McCarthy era, Robeson had recently re-emerged to resume his place in public life. We were excited to be able to perform for him.

With the near-death experience in Africa still fresh in our minds, many troupe members were afraid to get on a plane again, and requested that we not fly home. The director accepted our request, and we boarded a Soviet cruise ship from London to Leningrad on August 1. We stopped at ports in Norway, Denmark, Sweden and Finland, where we were allowed to go ashore. On a tour bus in Stockholm, when the tour guide told us that the government provided full healthcare to all citizens, someone said quietly, "Liar. Only a socialist country like China would provide such services. How could a capitalist country like Sweden supply public health services to all?"

London, 1960: Meeting singer Paul Robeson was
a highlight. He is in the center of the group; I
am second from the left in the front row.

We did not know why, but the relationship between China and the Soviet Union had deteriorated while we were on our trip, and the Chinese consulate in Leningrad had been withdrawn. Several Chinese students, at the request of the Chinese embassy in Moscow, welcomed us at the pier. The scheduled three-day visit was canceled and we were to take the night train to Moscow, but Leningrad was the cradle of the October Revolution, and we took advantage of the late sunset to have a quick look at the city. Anchored on the River Neva we saw the cruiser *Aurora,* from which the first cannon of the October Revolution was fired, sending Marxism and Leninism on a path that would lead to China's revolution.

The student who accompanied us was very keen to show us the sculpture of Peter the Great sitting on a horse, his eyes gazing to the west. The rear legs of the horse were trampling on a snake, which symbolized the conservative powers. The sculpture was saying that for Russia to become strong, it must change, it must learn from the West. The student told us: "Both Peter the Great and Japan's Meiji Restoration are good examples of nations becoming strong through learning from the West." This was not the type of thing we would commonly hear back in China!

When we returned to Moscow, the tombs of Lenin and Stalin were no longer open to the public. The reason, we were told, was that Stalin's body would be moved to the outskirts of the city. Actually, soon after we returned to China, we learned that the Soviet Communist Party had decided to remove Stalin's body and have it cremated as part of the de-Stalinization process. Global alignments were changing before our very eyes.

The domestic railway in the Soviet Union had nothing to recommend it. The train was slow and swayed violently throughout the nine tedious days from Moscow to Beijing. The one event that broke the boredom happened at a small station in the far east of the most beautiful social system in the world. … An old lady in rags on the platform approached our compartment and, extending her hand through the train window, begged for money. She was pushed back by the staff. We were amazed: "There are beggars in the Soviet Union? In theory, there shouldn't be any!"

Our question found its way to the ears of our leaders, and the director instructed us: "No one is to discuss and broadcast this after arriving home, as it concerns the image of the Soviet Union in the minds of the Chinese people."

We had to get off at Zabaykalsk, a city at the Chinese border, to change trains because the railway gauges were different. An old Chinese man started a conversation with us. He said he came to Zabaykalsk in the old times from the north of China to find his elder brother, but before he was able to find him, the October Revolution broke out, and he joined the Bolsheviks. He was very brave in battle and received a Lenin Award. He showed us a newspaper with a photo of him and Lenin. We discovered, however, that the old man, so respected in the past, dared not go back to his poor hometown in China, for his relatives now depended on him staying here to receive his pension.

The train traveled past the separation zone on the border, where there was a heavy military presence, something we had not seen when entering any other country. We were told that "All socialist countries are like brothers, and the relationship between China and the Soviet Union is unbreakable," but the reality was that each was cautious of the other. I could not understand what was wrong, but clearly something was not right.

9

A NEW PAIR OF EYES

After eight months of traveling the world, I returned home with a new pair of eyes. Before our departure, all seemed to be prospering. When we returned in September 1960, we were met with what would become a three-year disaster.

On the train back to Beijing, I shared a luxury cabin with soft beds with a Chinese boy from France called Qiu Xinghuang, who was going to study in Beijing. Since we were of a similar age, we quickly became friends, and members of the troupe started to tell him about the great achievements of our socialist country. But when we arrived in Beijing, Xing couldn't believe the lack of basic supplies. Daily necessities such as toilet paper, matches and salt were rationed, with long queues of people waiting to obtain them. He later told me sadly, "They lied to me on the train."

"They didn't know," I replied. "When we left Beijing in January, all looked good. Really. In May, when we were in Guinea, Shanghai's deputy mayor, Jin Zhonghua, also told us that the situation in China was excellent. You really shouldn't blame the members of our troupe. They were just like me—while we were spending time in Africa, we didn't know what was happening in China."

On our return we had to continue touring, performing widely throughout China. In one town, while I was queuing outside an eatery to buy my breakfast, a skinny man with a yellowish, sick complexion came over. He was very dirty and smelled awful. He approached a man at the next table and said, "Honorable sir, have pity on me. I haven't eaten for several days now. Please allow one bite for me."

"Get lost!" the other man cried. "I don't even have enough to eat myself. Why should I give anything to you? As a matter of fact, the food ration certificates I am using today are a result of saving here and there over a long time. I don't know anyone who would be kind enough to provide a few certificates so that I can have a big meal. You, as a man, don't work, and you want to beg. Shame on you."

The beggar said in a low voice, "I have no choice. My parents starved to death. I have nothing to eat, and that's why I am begging. And I have a permit issued by my work team, my brigade and the commune to allow me to beg for food. See, it's genuine."

"What, a level three permit?" The man at the table was growing impatient.

"You don't believe me? Look."

Watching this beggar, with a poster on the wall behind him showing Mao Zedong's words "Our party is glorious, great and correct," my mind flashed back to a speech I had heard at the time of the Great Leap Forward in 1958. Our team leader had praised the troupe for performing six sessions a day, which was a record.

"What was the audience attendance?" someone asked.

The team leader became very embarrassed and said, "Most people have gone to make steel, so the rate was not ideal." He swiftly changed the subject and described how the leaders at the local propaganda department had come to visit them. "We always think that an ideal society is far out of our reach. But the Central Committee of the Party has said that now that we can eat for free at the people's commune, we have actually entered Communism."

Remembering this, and witnessing the scene with the beggar just two years later, I felt embarrassed and worried.

*　*　*

While acrobatics was not the profession I would have chosen, in China we did as the party ordered. The African tour gave me a priceless chance to consider what I should do with my life. I couldn't change what job the party gave me, but I could make that job better. The trip had made me realize the uniqueness of my profession, and its role in foreign diplomacy, which enabled me to escape from a closed world and to see some of the wonders outside. My attitude toward my profession started to change.

The one sentence that made acrobatics my career for life was this: "Whoever is able to perform a handstand equal to that of Lauzik Malgit will be China's hero."

Zhang Guochu, the head of Beijing's Cultural Bureau, said this after seeing the Hungarian acrobatic troupe perform in Budapest. Though I had not seen Malgit myself, some of my colleagues had, and his handstand became legendary among our troupe. When I heard Zhang's words, I made a vow to become the best acrobatic performer of our time and chose the task of handstand, to surpass Malgit and become China's hero. I obtained a photograph of his handstand, which I used for inspiration.

In 1961, once I formally graduated from the acrobatic school, I became a full-time performer with the Shanghai Acrobatic Troupe. I applied for a one-year program of specialized circus training, ostensibly to learn horse riding, but with a personal plan to carve out more time to practice my handstand. Obsessed with the handstand, I would not alter my disciplined, intensive daily practice for anything.

Without doubt, I had chosen one of the hardest tricks. While doing a handstand it was hard to breathe, hard to balance, hard to maintain strength in your arms and body. This was why so few performers chose it as their specialty, and most who tried it gave it up: it was so hard! But because it was so obviously difficult, audiences would always value it.

The circus team training ground was at Chengjiaqiao on the western outskirts of Shanghai, surrounded by farming lands, with a deserted rail track to the north and an air force base to the west. On my first day there, March 5, 1962, a truly shocking incident took place that upset all my expectations and plans.

March in Shanghai was still cold, with rains soaking the earth and our mood. Because of the geographical inconvenience of the training ground, we all lived there. We had to get up at first light. While we were washing, a newly appointed lion trainer named Zhang Dexi asked me for toothpaste as he had forgotten his. That would be the last thing he would say to me.

At six, when we were doing our warm-up exercises, we heard someone screaming from the animal-training section.

"Tragedy! Tragedy! The tiger has mauled someone to death! The tiger has mauled someone to death!"

We ran fearfully toward the tiger cage, where we saw Zhang motionless on the floor, covered in blood. One tiger had gnawed on Zhang's right shoulder and was tugging at it, while the other was chewing his knee.

Outside the cage it was absolute chaos. Some people were using a long bamboo pole to poke one of the tigers, while others shouted at the top of their lungs, trying to scare the tigers away. Having tasted fresh human flesh, the tigers—which, until then, had been fed only thoroughly washed meat—had no intention of responding to the commotion and went on gnawing on Zhang. The tiger trainer finally arrived, entered the cage and used an iron spear to poke the tigers. He had trained and beaten them, and they obeyed him, dropping Zhang's body and reluctantly following the instruction to go into another cage. We were then able to enter the cage and move Zhang.

With Zhang's blood everywhere, it was a horrifying scene. An old man who was in charge of feeding the horses pushed his knee against Zhang's back to keep his lungs open. I used my left hand to hold up Zhang's pale bearded chin and my right hand to throw blood-clotting powder on the four holes left by the tigers' fangs. However, blood still streamed out, washing away the medication. The flow gradually stopped, but then Zhang ceased to breathe.

The old man placed Zhang on the cold cement floor and shut Zhang's eyes, which had been scratched by the tigers' claws. I went back to the dormitory and got his blue coat to cover his body. The ambulance took a long time to arrive. Afterwards, when I washed my hands, they were still covered with his blood. This was the first time I had been in contact with human blood, and I felt detached after the shock of it all. I was fifteen years old.

One minute, Zhang had said to me that he had forgotten to bring his toothpaste; an hour later, he was dead. We gathered at the animal-training ground after the ambulance departed. The tigers were crouching, licking the blood on their claws, looking at us as if sizing up their next target.

The incident analysis session in the main hall took place that afternoon, under a heavy pall of sadness. Outside, the rain kept coming down as if Heaven itself was crying. Everyone was struggling to comprehend that Zhang was dead. Someone asked why the cage had only been latched, claiming that if there had been a proper lock, Zhang could not have entered. The head of the circus explained that our country was in difficulty and he could not find a lock through-out the whole of Shanghai, so a latch was all he could afford.

Someone else said that spring and autumn were difficult seasons for animals and that these two tigers, which had been kept in a small cage previously, had only recently been relocated to bigger cages, which could have unsettled them. Some thought the tigers had been wrongly put in the lion cage, as young lion cubs were scheduled to arrive that afternoon. Perhaps Zhang was, in his position as the new lion trainer, trying to drive the tigers into their own cage.

People kept offering the wisdom of hindsight, which dumb-founded me. I did not know what to say. I only thought that if there had been stricter regulations and a lock on the cage, Zhang would not have died. Now that he was dead, what was the point of arguing about it?

At the end of the analysis session, the captain passed on com-ments from Director Wang, the head of our troupe: "The tigers that mauled Zhang to death must be trained as usual. People will like to see them."

The conference hall fell silent. The captain waited for the tiger trainer's response. Everyone knew that tigers that had killed people could not be trained to perform. Those who insisted on this would be endangering more lives.

The trainer, who had bravely gone into the cage and driven away the tigers, was still in shock. If his iron spear had not scared them, and they had attacked him, he would have been the second victim that day. Besides, his girlfriend had been complaining, saying that it was a dangerous occupation, and that he smelled of the tigers. The trainer was silent, showing his contempt for Wang's decision.

That evening, when it was really quiet, we could hear the falling rain and the unlatched windows banging in their frames with the wind. If there were any strange noises, the person on night watch ran to the animal-training ground to see if anything was wrong. It was as if the whole area were loaded with ammunition, which could be ignited by one single spark. Zhang's horse missed its master. Its sad neighing in the night made us all shudder.

In the nights that followed his death, I would often find myself awakened by either the rain or the neighing of Zhang's horse. Zhang's death would replay in front of my eyes, unstoppably. The fear I had not felt at the time was rushing in now, with a vengeance. I was not scared of Zhang's bloodstained body, but I was scared of the tigers. What if they escaped from their cages? Ah, the only safe place, after the tigers had escaped, would be the cages! I would hide in the cage, I decided.

According to existing agreements, the Western Suburbs Zoo was to provide young animals for circus training, and they could not be returned to the zoo. Nevertheless, one week later, Wang's order was overturned and the two tigers responsible for Zhang's death went back to the zoo. It was against regulations, but their departure brought my sleepless nights to an end.

After I got over that terrible incident, I turned my mind inwards, to my private program of acrobatic drills. The rural environment was an ideal place to train without distraction.

I knew that to be number one, I had no alternative but to practice as often and hard as possible. The bigger question was who would train me? I had no idea where to start. What were the requirements? What would be the correct programs to follow? What equipment would I need? From five-thirty each morning, when I got up, to eight-thirty in the evening, my time was taken up by circus training, three meals, a scheduled after-lunch nap, and reading Marx. I spent the remainder of my time in a room practicing handstands.

Marx said, "There is no royal road to science, and only those who do not dread the fatiguing climb of its steep paths have a chance of gaining its luminous summits."

Shanghai, 1962: Here I am practicing equestrianism, aged fifteen.

Whenever I felt exhausted, or overwhelmed by the fear of failure, and doubted I could go any further, whenever I could not see any hope on the horizon, I would think of this maxim, muster my belief and keep going.

Without a coach, I set my own rules: more frequent training, higher standards and pushing myself close to the ultimate limits of human physiology by prolonging my handstands, on both hands and on each hand separately. If I fell without completing my set target for the day, this failure would drive me forward. By the end of each day, my exercise cloth would be soaked with my sweat, and I would be too tired to walk in a straight line. Sometimes, when I sat

Shanghai, 1962: One-arm planche push-up to handstand.

on my bed washing my feet, before I even had time to change my trousers, I would fall asleep until the next morning.

Acrobatic performances are elegant, so I paid great attention to attaining beauty in my movements. But what is beauty? Through painting, sculpture, dance, gymnastic performances, literature and music, especially classical European music, I intuited the elements of beauty. Then I used these elements to shape my handstand gestures. I did not have much theoretical knowledge, but, due to the artistic influences I had received over the years, I could feel what beauty was.

My self-designed training effected a transition from the impossible to the possible, and from frustration to success. But there is only so much you can achieve through instinct. Understanding physics could take me a step further. I approached the circus coach and borrowed books, translated from Russian, such as *The Mechanics of Human Motions* and *Human Anatomy,* which I studied over and over after training sessions until I started to have a better understanding of Mao Zedong's words in *On Practice:* "What is perceived cannot at once be comprehended. Only what is comprehended can be more deeply perceived. Perception only solves the problem of phenomena; theory alone can solve the problem of essence."

Through those science books, I came to understand the relationship between the centroid (the center of gravity), the pivot point and the area supported. In order to move left, a right move must take place; the same is true with the up and the down. The theory of force and counterforce is everywhere, and is the key to maintaining balance in motion—which was essential as I had to prepare myself not just for handstands, but for handstands on moving platforms or unicycles, while also juggling rings on my free hand or feet. I examined whether my moves and gestures were theoretically correct, which helped me make better progress in my training.

I believed that the goddess of luck would not bless me with success too easily. Each time I wanted something from her, there was a price to pay, but the reward was in direct proportion to my efforts. I became more and more confident that I would not suffer the fate of Sisyphus; that I would push the stone of my struggles to the top of the hill of success.

At the circus training ground, time flew past. As winter came, I achieved my breakthrough. Due to my stubborn self-belief, analysis of my movements, a growing appreciation of the principles of beauty, and all that hard work, I achieved what I had set out to do: become the first Chinese acrobat to perform a single arm handstand; do what Malgit had done, but better. Malgit could do a one-arm handstand while spinning four rings. I was able to do it with seven rings. I was alone when I first did it. I was thrilled beyond belief.

10

THE UNVEILING

In the spring of 1963, the Hungarian acrobatic troupe performed in Shanghai. To have a closer look at their acts and design elements, a few young Chinese performers were assigned to carry props and even perform. I was one of them, working under the instructions of a Hungarian director.

We had cultural misunderstandings from time to time. To beckon someone, the Chinese wave with their palm facing down, while westerners curl their index finger in a continuous motion with the palm up, which is considered impolite by the Chinese. Whenever the Hungarian director used the finger-curling gesture, we would pretend not to see, which upset him.

I was excited to see the great Lauzik Malgit perform. Wearing a small moustache, he was in his forties but still had an excellent command of the skills, and his strength was remarkable. With the brisk Hungarian national music playing in the background, his performance was an eye-opener; but privately, I knew I could do better.

As host, the Shanghai Acrobatic Troupe arranged a "rehearsal" at our practice hall to entertain the Hungarians. We performed similar pieces, effectively to compete with them and defeat what an official from the Friendship Association called "the minor revision-ists." My new handstand was one of the items.

I neither understood nor cared about the conflict between China and the Soviets and their allies. I just wanted to perform well in front of my seniors and peers, and show that the Chinese were no worse than any other nation. The "rehearsal" went pretty well, and our Hungarian guests applauded our performances enthusiastically. My performance was better than theirs, but the "minor revisionists" didn't seem to feel defeated. It looked like the Chinese had worried too much.

Malgit and his wife both gave me a big congratulatory hug. I had had no experience of the human warmth in a hug, and here was one coming from strangers—and my idol! I was a bit lost, especially when Mrs. Malgit hugged me. I genuinely felt like a baby in her arms, wrapped in a very thick cotton blanket. They could have had no idea of the impact their kindness had on me.

During a break between the Hungarian performances, and with the assistance of an interpreter, I chatted to Malgit backstage. He belonged to the Hungarian Socialist Workers' Party. At the time of the Shanghai Acrobatic Troupe's visit to Hungary in 1956, he told me, the Hungarian Revolution was underway. He and the manager at the theater in which the Shanghai troupe was performing risked their lives to escort the Chinese acrobats to the border in two big buses displaying white flags. On the way back to Budapest, the manager was killed. Our conversation reminded me of the bullet holes in the walls in Budapest. My chest swelled with respect for Malgit's bravery.

After the Hungarian troupe left, we performed around China, including Beijing, where we met the Chongqing Acrobatic Troupe, which was about to embark on a visit to Sudan. Chongqing's cultural bureau director said they may not have the best acrobatic

Shanghai, 1963: My one-armed handstand with spinning rings.

performers in China, but their political correctness was unquestionable. When Director Wang repeated the Chongqing cultural bureau director's words to us, he voiced the hope that the Shanghai Acrobatic Troupe could also have "unquestionable political correctness."

Soon, however, the political correctness of the Chongqing Acrobatic Troupe came into question. A few days after arriving in Sudan, one of their performers jumped ship, becoming the first member of an acrobatic troupe to go AWOL during a diplomatic foreign visit. When interviewed by the Voice of America, he told how in Sichuan Province there was nothing to eat, nothing to wear, and people had been starving to death. News of this grave embarrassment spread quickly among our troupe.

While I was at the theater in Beijing, I received a call from Li Shi, the political counselor at the Chinese embassy in Sudan. He had liked my performance in Sudan very much, and wanted to see me.

Surprised to hear from him, I asked, "Uncle, why did you come back to China? How did you know how to reach me?"

Li Shi responded, "It was easy. I heard you are performing in Beijing, so I called the theater. As for the question of why I came back, we'll talk about it when we meet."

I asked for leave and went to a hotel run by the foreign ministry. Li Shi was unchanged after three years, still very friendly and energetic. After long exposure to the African sun, he had a ruddy glow.

"The young kid has grown up!" He patted me on the shoulder and said, "Have you heard about the incident with the Chongqing troupe? It was me who brought them back. That's why I came back so suddenly."

He said the Chongqing troupe had performed at the same theater where we performed in Khartoum. Since we had left, the Sudanese had built a hotel nearby, where the Chongqing troupe enjoyed far better accommodation. However, at their very first public performance, when the curtain was raised for the jar juggling and the music played, there was no performer. The crowd became restless. Members of the troupe went searching for the jar juggler, but there was no trace of him either backstage or at the hotel. His Western-style suit was found discarded on a chair at reception, which meant that there was a plan, and that he had received assistance from outside. A few days later, news came that the juggler had applied for political asylum.

Since the Chongqing and Shanghai acrobatic troupes were both in Beijing, a joint performance was arranged with the China Acrobatic Troupe and the troupe from the Railway Services System. Our professional peers in Beijing came to watch the show, which became a friendly competition, with the audience judging the innovative developments, level of difficulty, the pressure on the performers, and the stagecraft. Everyone knew it would be a great feat to perform well under these circumstances.

Since I was still sixteen and unburdened by the expectations that some more famous adult performers had to carry, I was confident that I would perform well with my handstand. I had the spirit of a "young bull who is not afraid of a tiger," as the traditional proverb has it. I did perform well, doing my one-arm handstand on a raised platform while spinning rings on my free hand and both of my feet, demonstrating my ability to handle pressure. I could tell from the loud applause that all my training had not been in vain.

After that performance, I gained standing in China's acrobatic circles. Many years later, Xia Juhua, chairman of the Chinese Acrobatic Association, told me that when they were performing in the Soviet Union in 1957, they had thought it would be wonderful if a Chinese performer could do a handstand as well as the Soviets. I had fulfilled their hopes.

Each year on May 1, Labor Day would be celebrated with cultural activities for the masses in Tiananmen Square. In 1963, the Chinese Ministry of Culture arranged for the Shanghai Acrobatic Troupe to perform. Only the best were chosen and I was invited.

We departed at dusk, traveling through the closed-off streets and arriving early at the Gate of Heavenly Peace. The square before us was transformed by brilliant floodlights. From the Tiananmen rostrum, on top of the monumental gate, we saw people performing group dances, and were amazed by the fireworks display against the night sky. We felt the great happiness and festivity of our capital city. The highest leaders sat at round tables laden with fruit and snacks, watching the performances and fireworks. Chairman Mao did not come, so Premier Zhou Enlai walked among the tables, greeting the guests. I was immersed in the peaceful atmosphere on top of the gate, and made a promise to myself to perform well.

There were two stages on the gate, with dancers and singers on the west and acrobats on the east. The makeshift lighting system could only provide side lights, not the top spotlights we usually needed, which was a big disadvantage for me. The Ministry of Culture's chief of acrobatic performances, seeing the strong wind blowing the flags, asked me: "Are you confident? The wind is very strong, and the lighting is not perfect."

"Yes. Please rest assured. Tonight's performance is very important, and I will definitely perform well."

Shows can turn us all into starstruck children, and China's highest echelon was like any other audience, thrilled to applause when I stood on my hands.

After the celebrations, we were allowed to walk on top of the gate. As the leaders were leaving and we had started to pack up our props, I followed the railings to the main building of the gate. Seeing that no one was watching, I went to the center of the rail, where the chairman stood during an inspection, and paused there. I remembered an image from a patriotic documentary: an array of soldiers, 150 to each line, carrying their guns, marching past the spot where I stood. MiG-15 fighter jets soared above my head and I could hear the shouts of "Long Live! Long Live!" A sense of greatness arose in me.

There was a lift on the west side of the gate, for the leaders' use only. On the east side was a flight of stairs, up and down which we maneuvered our equipment. All that greatness disappeared completely as I made my way down with heavy boxes of props.

At the end of September, we traveled to Xuzhou, a city in Jiangsu Province. After a few days there, the Friendship Association ordered us to Shanghai to prepare to depart for the Games of the New Emerging Forces in Indonesia. The great haste suggested either an emergency or faulty organization. We were put under pressure: any loss due to the early termination of our contract would be the Friendship Association's responsibility, we were told.

After sweeping through Shanghai to prepare our costumes, supplies and props, we left for Beijing, where we underwent investigations and were briefed by Zhou Erfu, the director of the Friendship Association. The participants at the games were mainly anti-imperialist and emerging decolonized countries in Asia, Africa and Latin America. These splendid games would contrast with the imperialist-controlled Olympic Games being held in Tokyo. China has always used sport for political purposes. The political leadership determined who should and should not compete. Organization and discipline were vital, as was our understanding of our anti-imperialist purpose.

Zhou Erfu likened Indonesia to a dumbbell, weak in the middle and strong on both sides. President Sukarno was the middle part, the weak link between the Communist Party and the military, hence the situation was complex and dangerous. We needed to be well prepared. We rushed to Guangzhou in the south of China to meet the athletics team, and were kept in our rooms at the Yuexiu Hotel to study foreign affairs regulations and background material on Indonesia.

Tao Zhu, first secretary of the central-south region, came to the dock to see us off. There was a grand departure ceremony for us and the North Korean sports delegation and their song and dance troupe, with whom we were traveling on the vessel *Guang Hua*. The provincial leaders took on the arduous task of shaking hands with each and every member boarding the ship, which delayed our departure.

Premier Zhou Enlai attached great importance to our safety in light of a possible attack by the Taiwanese navy when we sailed through the Taiwan Strait at night. A strict blackout would be implemented, and we were told the South Sea Fleet, on high alert, would give us an escort.

Before the sun went down, the ship sailed on a calm turquoise ocean. As I stood on deck enjoying the wind blowing, seeing schools of fish jumping out of the water, I had a sudden insight into the natural environment that inspired our traditional poets. It was a pity that the feeling only lasted for a moment, before I turned to practice my daily drills on the deck and watch the sportsmen train. I saw a swimmer swimming really hard in a makeshift canvas "swimming pool," with a rope tied around his waist. I saw a cyclist pedalling fiercely on a stationary bicycle. I saw gymnasts practicing on their equipment on the heaving deck. I saw other athletes running, making good use of the space available.

The *Guang Hua* was a good place for me to meet people and talk, either on the deck or in the lounge. I was curious about the dozens of North Koreans but, apart from rehearsals on the deck, and sometimes in the lounge, we did not see any of them. Was their discipline even stricter than ours? The friendship between China and North Korea had been strengthened by blood in the Korean War, and there should have been better communication. I went to ask the Chinese gymnastic team, who had visited North Korea in 1962, what the country was like, and they told me that Sino-North Korea friendship was only a slogan. In North Korea, they had seen graves of our soldiers that had been vandalized The North Koreans said China did not come to their aid to fight off the Americans, but only to achieve its own ends.

No Taiwanese navy ships attacked us in the Taiwan Strait, and after a week at sea we arrived in Jakarta for what would be a 35-day visit. The Chinese and North Korean delegations were taken to the Games Village by twenty-five big official buses, with Indonesian military police cars in front. The sports delegations were allocated premises displaying Chinese national flags, while our troupe and the North Korean song and dance troupe were housed next to the Soviet Union's artistic troupe at the other end of the heavily guarded village.

My first impression of Jakarta was the extreme heat. Every day, we had frequent showers to cool our heads and maintain calm. Local Chinese people told us to eat more papaya to avoid constipation. In such heat, we all lost weight. Luckily, I had practiced in all types of hot and cold weather since I was young, and in all weathers in Africa, so I was able to adjust as quickly as anyone.

On the day of the opening ceremony, I saw soldiers with machine guns under each lamppost all the way from the Games Village to the sports ground. Armored vehicles full of soldiers patrolled the vicinity. There was a police presence inside the ground. It was like they were preparing for war. The newspaper reported that more than 10,000 military police had been mobilized to ensure the security of the opening ceremony.

Our performances went well. I was no longer the boy who had gone to Africa. Enthusiastic applause and screams of delight from the audience were the norm during my performances, which filled me with pride and satisfaction after so much hard work.

Whenever we entered the Games Village, we could hear the crowd shouting "GANEFO! GANEFO!" (Games of the New Emerging Forces). Often young Chinese-Indonesian girls waited outside the theater where we performed and, on spotting us, asked for autographs. My name was known in Jakarta and Bandung. We often performed to Indonesian songs such as "Sing Sing So," "Oh Mummy" and "River Solo," which were also popular songs in China, and the Chinese singer Liu Shufang performed "Butet," or "Daughter," which we loved. The song is about a mother with a baby daughter waiting for the father, a member of the Indonesian people's resistance against Dutch colonialists, to come home. In my memory, it goes something like this:

Baby, your dad is living in hardship
He has joined the militia to fight the enemy, my dear baby
Baby, don't be sad, my dear baby
Your mother and you will wait to hear from him
Go to sleep, my good baby, my baby
Our troops will definitely succeed and your dad will come
    home safe
Go to sleep, my good baby.

The song seemed a fine example of political correctness, but after one performance, an Indonesian Communist Party member came and gave us a dressing-down, saying it was a revisionists' song that couldn't generate a fighting spirit!

Our hosts had been too busy organizing security for the games to look after us elsewhere, but there was only one incident of note. Normally, when we were bussed to the theater, the main gate would be opened for our entrance. But one day, it was closed. We were about to protest, but an officer from the Chinese embassy gestured to us not to worry. He seemed to have dealt with this before. He took out two cartons of the famous Zhonghua cigarettes, gave an insincere smile and got off to negotiate. The "toll ticket" was effective and the main gate stayed open for us for the remainder of the trip.

On November 22, 1963, the American president John F. Kennedy was assassinated in Dallas. Many countries lowered their flags in the Games Village to half-mast in a sign of condolence, but the Chinese athletics team did not follow suit. I do not know what Vietnam and North Korea did. The Kennedy assassination taught me a hard fact: politics is dirty and horrible, and China was not going to compromise on its opposition to the imperialist West.

After the games, President Sukarno invited the athletics teams from various nations to the Independence Palace. It was our second visit to this huge, extremely grand palace after an earlier special performance for the president. We were surprised to see Dipa Nusantara Aidit, chairman of the Indonesian Communist Party, but he had good connections with the Chinese embassy. The deputy chairman of the Indonesian Communist Party also came, and read a poem opposing the Soviet Union's recommended path to power through parliamentary struggle, with the last line, "Don't sink in the mud," demonstrating the determination of their party to follow Chinese advice to take the path of armed revolution. We knew that by adopting this stance the Indonesian Communist Party, sandwiched between China and the Soviet Union, would further increase uncertainty for Indonesia. It was amazing to us that these opposition figures were tolerated within the president's own home, but, as we had been told, he was the "weak center" of the dumbbell, using all his skills to keep both the left and the right in equilibrium.

After the games, our Indonesian hosts arranged for us to perform in Bandung, an area controlled by the opposition rightists. There were warnings of bomb attacks, assassination and kidnap attempts against the Chinese, North Korean and Soviet Union troupes. The Soviet troupe had already been attacked. Our troupe's party committee urged us to be on high alert. "Appear normal while being very cautious" was the order. Four people would occupy a double room, two on the beds and two on the floor. Men would stay in alternate rooms, not together in a cluster, so they could provide assistance to the women should an emergency arise. In the evenings, the youth league affiliated with the Indonesian Communist Party would patrol outside our hotel, and sometimes stay on our floors as an extra precaution.

Despite the tension, our Bandung performances were a great success. Only at the last show was there a small incident, when some people who could not get a ticket broke the cordon and turned the theater into chaos. Our performance had to stop. Had the rightists done something? we wondered. Luckily, it was only our popularity causing the problem. We were eventually able to complete our performance, but we left Bandung in a hurry.

Back at the Games Village in Jakarta, I went onto the balcony to observe the neighboring North Korean and Soviet troupes. While the North Korean troupe had heeded warnings from the Chinese and avoided attacks by the Indonesian rightist forces, many of the Soviets wore bandages and dressings, making the Games Village feel more like a field hospital.

Sailing back through the South China Sea on the *Guang Hua*, I felt the vastness and security of the South China Sea. A Shanghai

Jakarta, 1963: Our visit to Independence Palace was memorable. Dipa Nusantara Aidit, chairman of the Indonesian Communist Party, is in the second row from the front, sixth from the left. I am in the back row, the first on the right.

Bandung, 1963: Our shows were a huge hit. Here, I am the performer on top.

105

navy veteran saw me standing on the deck, enjoying the view. He pointed out the islands and told me which ones were occupied by the People's Liberation Army and which were occupied by the KMT. Some islands were occupied by both sides, apparently in peace, a symbol of China's sovereignty and unity, a cause which ironed out all internal divisions. I was about to be drawn into that effort deeper than ever before.

11

IN THE ARMY

In July 1965, we were called into a meeting at the troupe compound. Director Wang announced, "The party requires all people over eighteen years to spend time in the Liberation Army. Men will go first, then the women. You will go for two weeks."

I thought it would be like a two-week camping trip. We were sent out to Wujiaochang, to a training brigade affiliated with the Shanghai Public Security Bureau, to "learn from the army" and to "unify revolutionary thoughts." Our day started at five-thirty in the morning to the sound of the military bugle, and ended at nine-thirty in the evening with another bugle. The day was filled with exercises such as hand-to-hand fighting, shooting and bayonet fighting.

For meals, we had to march to the dining hall, loudly singing military songs. Within fifteen minutes, we had to gulp down whatever we could lay our hands on, because the activity continued after dinner. Sometimes, even after the lights-out bugle, we were not allowed to sleep, as a study session or an emergency drill would be called. We would be rushed to the outskirts of the city for a "search" exercise, chasing imaginary enemies until it was nearly daybreak. The wake-up bugle would blast before we were able to sleep. We were at full alert at all times. Because my training in the acrobatic troupe had a pseudo-military rigor, I was quite tough and able to adjust.

Realizing that it could be useful to have some skills in fighting, I became fully engaged. "Temples on the head, private parts down there, ribs on the sides, and heart in the middle" were the points on the body we learned to attack with bayonets. I enjoyed shooting, and gained a score of 55 out of 60 for 100-yard shooting using a Type 56 assault rifle, which ranked me number one in our group.

During these two weeks, the battalion chief was very busy, whereas the commissar in charge of political thought took things easy, failing to conduct a single political lesson. We had two talks from the public security bureau which were counted as political lessons, but the brigade leaders were eager to hear our suggestions for improving their work. In our debrief with them, seeing that everyone was smiling and not talking, to break the ice I said, "Some ideological work for a mere two weeks, to form a pair with a soldier, so that 'Two soldiers help each other to become a "red" pair'. . . . Is this a little artificial?"

The leaders seemed embarrassed. My heart missed a beat. Damn, I had said something wrong. After the meeting, our troupe leader scolded me: "You! I don't know what to say to you. You only know your practices and drills, you know nothing about subtlety in society. The purpose of us coming to the brigade was to learn from them. How could you think of their shortcomings? And, even worse, voice it at the meeting! It was only a polite gesture when the leader asked us to provide comments and suggestions. Just like in every work unit, there is a notebook for all to provide feedback. But should you make real comments? No! A lot of things in the world are to be viewed from upside down. How ironic that you are the one who is practicing being upside down, and you do not know about this!"

That was a very interesting lesson. It did give me a totally new angle from which to observe the world!

After fourteen days, we packed our humble belongings and bade farewell to our training mates, who had come from ten different posts in Shanghai.

"Jingjing, how I envy you," one of them said. "You have been a soldier for only two weeks, and you can already retire. We have been here for four years, and we have to get through another year before we can retire."

"One year will pass very quickly," I said without thinking.

"Quickly to you; but to us, it will be very slow," a soldier from Shanghai said.

Military life, I knew from just two weeks' exposure, was boring. I could understand how frustrating it would be for an ambitious young man to spend his best years in the army, then have to find a job. Even my fourteen lost days of training time felt like a lot to me. I thought I could make it up after returning to the troupe, but no sooner were we back in Shanghai than we were sent, with the female acrobats, to Military Unit 6403 in the Zhoupu district—for a whole month! I was extremely frustrated. My dream was to become a world-class acrobat, which required continual practice and regular training. I had already lost two weeks and was about to lose another four. But what could I do? In a country where politics is paramount, all must serve political needs.

Zhoupu was not far from Shanghai, and we were assigned to a howitzer artillery unit. We undertook military training just like the full-time soldiers, and felt lucky to get good care and food. I was allocated to a wireless communications squad. The squad leader, from Nanjing Military Region, was a well-known activist who had more or less memorized Mao's works and was the only party representative in the battalion, so he had the world at his feet. I realized I had been

Shanghai, 1965: Me performing the reversed heaven and earth.

assigned there so that I could be influenced by this model "Red expert" to follow the path of the party loyalist, about which I had no idea. Being with the squad leader all day every day, I was meant to learn to keep up with political trends in revolutionary times, but I was not cut out for such things. The guiding principle firmly rooted in my head was: on stage, perform as well as you can; off stage, be as honest a man as you can. I was only ambitious to perform handstands, not to acquire political status, and hoped the month would pass quickly. Time was precious for me. But these principles were contrary to the expectations of the leaders of our troupe. Unwittingly, by ignoring this attempt at indoctrination I was putting my future in jeopardy.

The equipment used at Military Unit 6403 was obsolete, mostly relics from the Second World War. The two walkie-talkies were the kind used in the Korean War. Upon seeing our disappointed faces, the company commander, fully understanding, said, "What you are seeing now are weapons for training purposes. Once a war breaks out, there will be new weapons ready for use."

It would take time to learn how to use new artillery, so I didn't know what was to be gained from training with old equipment. Of course, I thought too much. At that time, the battalion had achieved No. 1 political status, and had won "Four-good Battalion" and "Five-good Soldier" awards (meaning "good in politics"). Politics, not performance, had an impact on everything, and politics was the heart and soul of what the army did.

After the revolutionary military hero Lin Biao took over the role of defense minister in 1959, he launched the study of the selected works of Mao. Lin Biao said, "The Three Old Essays should be studied, not only by the soldiers but also by our cadres. It may be easy to simply read these three essays, but not so easy to act accordingly. These essays must be studied so that they become everyone's mottos."

Sitting on one's bum and studying the three essays—"Serve the People," "In Memory of Norman Bethune" and "The Foolish Old Man Who Moved the Mountain"—over and over could not be more boring, but no one could let this show on their face. Feeling time dragging, I kept checking my watch, which seemed to be refusing to tick. When the squad leader glowered at me, I put my head down and pretended to keep reading.

Those political classes were ad hoc, without course outlines or plans. Most of the soldiers, from rural areas, were uneducated and obedient. Each wanted to be a five-good soldier, so that they could be selected to become a member of a party cadre. Questioning the nature of the political materials was not on their minds.

The one person with actual military experience was the political instructor, who had joined the army in 1947, during the civil war. He told us that wars, especially modern wars, were cruel. They were not like the ones shown in movies, where the enemy always suffers more losses. "Out of fifty people who joined the army in my village," he told us, "only three are still alive."

Army life could be cruel in peacetime, too, as many soldiers discovered. Once, the political instructor asked a soldier who had just come from a rural area: "Who is Song Qingling?"

"Sir, I don't know."

"Song is the deputy chairman of our country. Do you know if Song is a male or a female?"

The soldier's mind ticked. In his hometown in the north of Jiangsu Province, males dominated families; all leaders were male, apart from the position of director of the women's committee. How could the deputy chairman of our country be a woman?

"Male."

"Wrong. Song is a female."

Everyone laughed at the soldier's answer. The instructor followed with another question.

"Is Bai Qiu En a Chinese or foreign doctor?" (Bai Qiu En was the Chinese name given to Henry Norman Bethune, a member of the Communist Party of Canada, who had been turned into a hero of internationalism by Mao.)

"Chinese."

"Why?"

"Because his family name is Bai," the soldier answered with much confidence.

"Wrong. He's a foreigner, a Canadian. If you had studied Chairman Mao's article 'In Memory of Norman Bethune,' you'd have known he was a doctor, a Canadian Communist who came from thousands of miles away to China to assist in fighting the Japanese invaders."

These incidents of ridicule peppered the boring days of army life.

That year, 1965, saw many wars in Asia. The prolonged Vietnam War still felt closer to its beginning than its end. In August, a second war broke out between India and Pakistan. Following a decision by the party's Central Committee, Chinese troops started to prepare for possible action by learning English. A squad leader was sent to regimental headquarters to receive training. Upon his return, he wrote "Get your hands up" on the blackboard. Then, in order to help the soldiers learn to pronounce this sentence, he added Chinese characters. The line read like this: "Gait'er You'er Hanz, erPoo," and all, including me, learned this classic phrase which would be useful on the battlefield. However, before we could say it in an understandable form, India and Pakistan had stopped fighting.

The army was supposed to have China's National Day off, on October 1. A notice came out: 5 percent of the soldiers could apply for leave, and the rest had to stay behind. As a short-term cadet, I had no choice. The commander mobilized us to do voluntary work. The pigsty, a sideline business of the military unit, became the focus of these good deeds. The unlucky pigs could not enjoy their sleep anymore, as every hour a group of soldiers came to clean the pigsty. What could we do? There were more soldiers than pigs. One soldier from Shanghai who did not get the chance to clean the pigsty complained: "Even the pigs live in Communism today."

Another unlucky soldier said: "I don't think so. The pigs would be upset because their lives have been severely interrupted. If they could, they would lodge a complaint."

I had no wish to participate in the pigsty cleaning. It was a public holiday, and there was nothing to do. I thought I might as well read the *Liberation Daily*—the only newspaper allowed, which was placed on a special hanger on the wall where everyone would fight to get their hands on it. That day, the paper reported the so-called September 30 incident, in which the Indonesian Communist Party suffered a merciless crackdown from the right-wing military. Not only did the Indonesian Communist Party not get the power they were seeking, but many were murdered or detained. The worst-case scenario, which had been in the back of my mind since returning from Indonesia, had come to pass.

After my long month in the army, I had not learned much, but eventually I was able to "retire." Soon after I returned to Shanghai, the troupe's Communist Youth League representative came to persuade me to join.

"All youth seeking advancement should join the Youth League," he said, "and you will progress under the assistance of the league. Someone like you, who is professionally diligent and politically clean, should be proactive and apply to become a member."

I filled in the application form and, within a month, was

approved. It was later that I came to understand that it was fixed in advance: if the league wanted you, you always got to join, but if they did not want you, no matter how proactive you were, you could never join.

At the solemn official ceremony, I was totally confused by the words "To strive my whole life for the Communist cause." These words appeared on my application form at the request of the recommender, against my will. My becoming a Youth League member was meant to demonstrate that I was seeking advancement, but I had not read a single book about Communism and really did not know what kind of "ism" it was, or what kind of society was the ideal society for human beings. I had heard of its distribution principle, "To each according to his need." Apart from this, I knew nothing other than the empty slogans I was taught to parrot. How could I know that I wanted to strive my whole life for a cause about which I had no knowledge? Was I not cheating myself as well as others? When reading my vows, I was ashamed of the sound of my voice.

In March 1966, the Communist Party office invited me to join the party. Once invited, refusal would be frowned upon. I thanked the party from the bottom of my heart for their intention to cultivate me. In a society where "if there was no Communist Party, there would not be the new China," being a party member was a must for good social status. Otherwise, no matter how talented you were, you would achieve nothing. Everyone in China knew this, including me. And yet I found myself unable to accept. The shame I had felt at the Youth League ceremony was lingering in my heart. In my mind, a party member should be someone who would be at the forefront in the event of danger or difficulty, and would be willing to sacrifice his life. That was not me. Anything less would be cheating them. I knew I did not deserve to be a party member when I scrutinized myself from different angles.

So I confessed to the person who invited me: "I am very far away from the standard of being a party member. However, I will use these standards as my yardstick, and I want the party to observe me and test me."

My honest words were interpreted as disobedience, and they disregarded me from then on. It was a near miss between me and party membership, but I did what I did for the right reasons and my mind was at peace. I did not yet understand what it would cost me.

12

THE SWIRL OF
THE CULTURAL
REVOLUTION

A cult-creating movement was speeding ahead at full throttle. I, like the rest of the population, was fully involved in the passionate worship of a new god.

Later, when I learned about the recent history of the world, I found that similar god-creating movements had ended tragically for the populace where they had taken place. To worship a leader of a country is a negation of the value of people's lives. China's movement to idolize Mao Zedong, to worship him as the "Sun," was no exception. On the one hand, I thought Mao was a great leader; on the other, I didn't understand the rhetoric of the Cultural Revolution—it was against all my experience and beliefs. I felt the contradictions, but I still found myself revering this human being as a god.

The "smashing of the Four Old Things," which the radicals in the party set in train, reviled Chinese cultural and ethical values backed by thousands of years of tradition. Through the Red Guards movement, the party called on China's youth to deride old culture, old habits, old ideas and old customs, and replace them with worship of Mao, who took advantage of those innocent, restless, passionate young minds and converted their zeal into a destructive social force.

With the support of Mao and the Central Cultural Revolution Group, young Beijing Red Guards holding a big banner reading "Long Live the Red Terror!" rushed south to Shanghai to implement the smashing of the Four Olds. They raided civilian houses, imprisoned accused capitalists and intellectuals, and even burned civilian book collections. What the Red Guards smashed was our excellent cultural heritage, piece by piece. In scale, the Four Olds movement dwarfed the excesses of Qin Shi Huang, the first emperor of China, who burned books and buried alive some Confucian scholars.

Francis Bacon said, "knowledge is power." In the Cultural Revolution, human civilization turned backward. A young person like myself ought to have been seeking knowledge, but I was not able to acquire any reading materials. The only books I was allowed to read were the selected works of Marx, Engels, Mao and Lu Xun, the famous Chinese poet and essayist.

Burning books was just the beginning. Included in the list of the Four Olds was the Hongqiao Cemetery, where the tombs of the parents of Song Qingling—wife of Dr. Sun Yat-sen, the founding president of the Republic of China—could be found. I could not believe it when I heard this. I jumped on my bicycle and pedalled to Hongqiao, where I was dumbfounded to see headstones broken and tilted, cover stones lifted and dropped, red-satin shrouds torn and bones strewn everywhere. The Songs' headstone was nowhere to be found.

At the end of 1966, to prepare for the unique stage performance of a revolutionary drama created by Jiang Qing, *Madame Mao*, the leftist branch of the Cultural Revolution stooped so low that they even had revolutionaries attacking opera houses. The excuse was that the operas shown there were bourgeois "sinister line" arts, and no traditional performance was allowed, nor any creation of new artwork, nor even rehearsal or practice. Only Madame Mao's shows were allowed.

What I could not understand was why a cultural revolution needed to label excellent traditional Chinese culture as feudalism, universal humanitarian thought as capitalism, and the understanding and interpretation of Marxism-Leninism by the Soviet Communists as revisionism.

In China, whenever there was a revolution, the difference between right and wrong became blurred. Back in the Anti-Rightist Campaign of 1957, a percentage of the people had to be categorized as rightists, without any proper process of identification. Above all else, the party wanted a revolution and if it could not find enemies, it would invent them. The Cultural Revolution was the same game, only the underdogs were now the top dogs, and many of the tortured became the torturers.

The delicate and tranquil courtyard of the acrobatic troupe did not escape the Cultural Revolution. Even the goldfish in the pond became a target of revolutionaries, who decided they were a symbol of old traditions. With the fish gone, mosquitoes drove all of us behind nets in summer. The stone lions were smashed. The cobblestone path was also destroyed and became a muddy, squashy mess after rain. The two tablets with beautiful characters written on them were covered with cement. In the pavilion, a pair of couplets was smeared with ink; the stone tables and stools were overturned and thrown aside. Posters bearing accusations against so-called "cow demons and snake spirits" (terms used for enemies of the revolution) written in large Chinese characters appeared on the walls of our exercise building and the administrative office. These big-character posters were a constant reminder to us of the ferocity of the Cultural Revolution being waged throughout the country.

The January Storm, which started in early 1967 in Shanghai and then rippled across the whole of China, was a coup single-handedly masterminded by Mao Zedong to purge those comrades who had fought with him in the early years. Most notable among them was Liu Shaoqi, the former president of China, who was denounced for opposing Mao, placed under house arrest, and paraded at humiliating public denunciation meetings. Some leaders believed they would "rather commit political error than commit organizational error"; they too were classified by Mao Zedong as "capitalist roaders," a crime they were beaten and intimidated into confessing.

Riding the January Storm, the radicals in our troupe took power. To perform with the troupe, apparently, would stall the progress of the Cultural Revolution, and whoever was seen practicing would be considered a saboteur. Hence, my practice stopped. In such an environment, where no one dared to practice, and no performance was allowed, my dream of climbing to the top of the world acrobatic community and of glorifying our country had suddenly evaporated. This affected me severely. The frustration was beyond description, putting me near the edge of collapse, and because nobody could be trusted, I had no one to talk to about this. I was devastated and alone.

The radicals formalized their takeover of the troupe by seizing its official seal, or signature stamp. For thousands of years, a seal has been the symbol of power in China. Taking the seal meant they could capture Director Wang, the head of our troupe.

Settling accounts with capitalist roaders in "struggle sessions" was the best way for the radicals to demonstrate their loyalty to Mao Zedong. These episodes of public humiliation and torture allowed the radicals to vent their anger and legitimize their seizure of power.

They tirelessly carried out struggle sessions against Wang and paraded him in the streets. They held his arms back and pushed his head down to form a "plane" position, then assaulted and abused him, destroying what was left of his self-confidence.

The struggle sessions in our troupe were held in the dining hall. A portrait of Chairman Mao hung high above the leaders of the radical group sitting, stern-faced, on the stage. In the front row were supportive radicals. Behind them were the middle-grounders who supported whoever was in power. Behind them, I was among the others who sat or stood, ignoring whatever the radicals were saying, resentful about having to attend such sessions.

The struggle sessions followed set routines. First, all were to rise and sing the "Internationale":

> There are no supreme saviors
> Neither God, nor Caesar, nor tribune
> Producers, let us save ourselves,
> Decree the common salvation.
> So that the thief expires,
> So that the spirit be pulled from its prison.
> Let us fan our forge ourselves,
> Strike while the iron is hot.

And then, "The East Is Red":

> The East is red,
> The sun rises.
> From China arises Mao Zedong.
> He strives for the people's happiness,
> Hurrah, he is the people's great savior!

Then we shouted the words of vice-chairman of the CCP and defense minister Lin Biao:

> Long live the invincible Mao Zedong's thoughts!
> Long live our great leader Chairman Mao! Long live!

And then we'd sit down as someone shouted, "Bring up Wang, the counter-revolutionary revisionist!"

Wang, his name written upside down on a huge heavy blackboard, a red cross over each character, would be pushed up onto the stage, his arms held high from behind by two radicals in their khaki pseudo-military uniform, wearing armbands. Wang cooperated by bending his body forward at a 90-degree angle, and listened as they criticized him. As the person being "struggled," he had no chance to argue or defend himself.

In one of the sessions against Wang, there was a special guest, the wife of Zhang Dexi, the lion trainer who had been mauled to death. Ever since that terrible morning, the Zhang family had been grief-stricken and living in poverty. Zhang's wife's testimony revived my memories of his tragic death. Wang's crime was insisting on training dangerous tigers and, worse still, allowing such animals to perform for the purpose of attracting larger audiences. The tigers were sent back to the zoo, but many people had not forgotten Wang's actions.

Zhang's wife was the chief accuser in this struggle session. At the time of Zhang's death, she had been pregnant with their daughter. They also had a one-year-old son. Her mental health deteriorated severely after her husband's gruesome death, and she lost the ability to think properly or perform daily functions. It was an unusually quiet and peaceful struggle session, as everyone present, irrespective of their faction, listened to this frail woman's accusations. The heartless tiger-training program and the ignorance of the needs of the victim's family infuriated the audience.

"Labor transforms humans. Labor is of the utmost glory" was the motto that had been drummed into me since I was young. For his labor punishment, Wang was sent to the "cowshed."

In this unprecedented revolution, many new terms had been created, "cowshed" being one of them. Cow was short for "cow demons and snake spirits," and the shed was an informal prison for housing such targets of the revolution. Our cowshed was originally the storage room for our performing gear. It was made of bamboo poles and flimsy asphaltic felt which did not prevent the wind from entering. Shanghai in January was cold, with temperatures dropping to 20 degrees, and water droplets would turn to ice in no time. Wang was pushed into the freezing cowshed and told to confess to being a capitalist roader. Stripped of power, he lost his dignity and nodded timidly.

Wang had been a hard taskmaster himself, sending others to the cowshed, including Mo Feixian, a magician accused of being a KMT spy. Mo was still being held there when Wang was brought in. Mo looked at Wang through the spectacles balanced on his acne- and rosacea-marked nose, and said, "You also came?"

Wang told me later that on seeing Mo, the blood rushed to his head. He was too embarrassed to speak. It was at this time that he remembered what his mother had told him when he was little: "We must treat others well. Good deeds will have good consequences, and bad deeds, bad ones. The world is fair to everyone, for there is a consequence waiting for each deed performed."

The demoted Wang had to clean the toilet and the courtyard every morning in his torn winter clothing. After this, he had to sit in the cowshed and cudgel his mind, writing his confessions with a hand that could not hold the pen for frostbite. Cold winds blew from the west, brushing violently against the big-character posters.

Drips of water turned into icicles on outdoor taps. Wang, who had thought he was quite clear in his thinking when he was troupe director, could not come to terms with his situation. One day he had thought he was walking on the great thoroughfare of socialism, and the next, to his total bewilderment, he had slipped into the pit of capitalism. All his years of devotion to the party had been in vain; worse, it was considered evidence of his traitorous capitalist roader activities. He did not know how to start his confession. I went to the cowshed to try to comfort him and boost his morale. He just sat in the corner and avoided my eye.

*　*　*

Naively, I had immersed myself in my personal ambition to show through my performances that China could catch up to and outstrip the advanced world. I thought my dedication showed my patriotism. But while I concentrated on this goal, I ignored criticisms that had been piling up against me.

I was summoned to a struggle session. I had prepared myself for this possibility, but when my name was mentioned I felt very uncomfortable. Anticipating what might happen to me was the worst. I imagined that the feeling was like that of an animal hearing the whipping sound of the trainer's cane. I steeled myself by thinking back to the punishment I had suffered as a child. When the cane actually hit my skin, the fear disappeared. As long as I could handle it, it would be over soon. In my struggle session, I was called various names: "favorite pet of the dark line and revisionist artist," "extreme individualist pursuing personal achievements," "seeker of bourgeois benefits and fame" and "specialist yet not politically correct." None of them really meant anything, but there was a predetermined outcome. For "rehabilitation," I, along with others, was sent to the countryside for "chai zhu xie," or breaking up pig manure.

My task was straightforward. Pig droppings had been collected and piled up and left on the soil to ferment to become fertilizer for the next spring. When the time came, the farmers would use a bamboo pole with a basket on each end to carry the compost to the fields. Now it was spring, and the farmers needed laborers. We were instructed to fill the heavy baskets with manure and balance the middle of the bamboo pole on our shoulder. When we got to the field, we used a hoe to dig a shallow ditch and then distributed the manure evenly. Before the manure could be spread we had to break up the lumps, a task normally completed with the hoe, but the farm leader said, "Comrades, in order to help shape your worldview better, we require you to break the pig manure using your hands, not the hoes. This is a test to see if you can endure the stinking smell and the dirty work."

We in the work crew were stunned, thinking it must be a joke. It wasn't. What else could I do but follow orders? I squatted in the pig manure. The putrid smell rushed up my nose and turned my stomach. I felt as if my whole body was full of the stench. I held my breath for a few seconds, and then put my hand gingerly into the black and sticky stuff, still fermenting, with worms wriggling in it. For the next few days, all we did was break up lumps of pig manure and spread them in the field. When we were carrying the baskets, the manure was close to my face. While I was squeezing and squashing the stinking manure in my hands, the farm leader would be saying that this was intended to cultivate the proletarian quality of not being afraid of smells and shit. No matter how hard we washed, the odor always lingered on the hands that held the rice bowl when we ate. I could not understand what such an unhygienic practice had to do with forming a better worldview.

Hygiene was instinctive to me, having been brought up in a city and trained in the acrobatic troupe. Once, when I saw the eleven year-old son of the farmer was not in the habit of washing his hands, I told him, "You are a big boy now, and you need to be hygienic. You need to wash your hands more often." Who would have thought that I might be putting myself in danger, with these words, of being reported for teaching the kid bourgeois thought?

Our agricultural work continued, and often took place in the most difficult conditions. In the hottest part of the summer, we were supposed to help harvest and plant new crops at high speed. We worked, ate and lived with peasant families. On one agricultural stint, the farmers were a couple in their sixties with eleven daughters and one son. They had wanted a son very badly, and kept trying until they got one. Because of the number of children in the household, they had no spare room for the three of us from the troupe, so we slept in a mud shed where they stored firewood. Without a window or door, there was only one small entrance wide enough for one person to pass through at a time. It was only a little more than head height, and it had barely enough space for the three of us to lie down.

Centipedes, spiders and other insects were already claiming the shed as home, so we had to spray pesticides and lay down some hay. With mosquito nets over us, it was stuffy and airless. The sound of frogs croaking from the bottom of their lungs kept me awake; so did pain. I had injured my left knee when riding a horse, and my right knee when I had been practicing on the springboard. I also suffered from other joint pains developed during training. When I was carrying a laden bamboo pole through the rice paddies, both my shoulder and my back hurt unbearably. It was hell, but I had to learn to cope.

* * *

Once I was back from the pig farm, my record was considered clean again. Soon I found myself, as so many did, flipped from one of the accused into one of the accusers.

In 1968 came the internal cleansing phase of the Cultural Revolution. The investigators had a specific target. Yi Ban, of the First Office of the Shanghai Revolutionary Committee (which formerly belonged to the Department of Propaganda), had formed a special investigation team to sniff out those performers who had participated in the 1948 consolation show for KMT soldiers.

As performers, we never had any say in who could be in our audience. We took orders and performed for our livelihood. Who would have thought, back at the time of liberation, that consolation shows could become crimes twenty years later? Many performing troupes, including ours, had participated in shows for KMT soldiers. Before the KMT retreated to Taiwan in 1949, some files recording the performers' names had been kept while others were destroyed.

Due to the grand scale of this investigation, there was a lack of manpower to do the work. The special investigation team required party and Youth League members to bulk out their numbers. I had never dreamed of being dragged into the special investigation team, but I was still nominally a member of the Youth League and resources were short, so I was conscripted.

The task of the special investigation team was to scrutinize those ranking above "head of detachment"—the name for the troupe leaders—to find out what else, apart from performing for the soldiers, they did. Were there any special agents of the KMT left behind on purpose? The KMT government expected to come back to the mainland one day, to suppress the Communist rebellion and save the country. Because of this, people on the mainland had been on constant high alert. In the 1950s, Mo Feixian, the former magician who was in the cowshed at the troupe, had undergone the first of his many arrests for being a suspected KMT agent.

The investigation team was divided into groups, going around the country to collect evidence of the smallest trace of any hidden KMT activity. The group I had been assigned to was dispatched to work with the acrobatic troupes in Nanjing, Beijing and Taiyuan. When we arrived in Taiyuan, we saw trucks rushing by, loaded with machine guns. Sounds of shooting came from the distance. There had been no such fighting in Shanghai. I wondered if the Cultural Revolution was becoming a military one.

Our inquiry into the Taiyuan Acrobatic Troupe was not difficult. We investigated one man who had performed in the consolation shows for the KMT and had also been a member of the KMT artillery. We looked for evidence of him creating problems in the troupe, but found nothing. After our task was completed, we needed to have our task certificate affixed with the official seal of the work unit. When doing so, I was aghast to find the seal bundled together with a hand grenade. I asked why. The person who was assisting us told me: "After the radicals took power in Taiyuan Acrobatic Troupe, there was an imbalance in the distribution of power. A fight broke out for control of the seal. Neither camp could win, so they came to a solution that the seal was to be kept by me, who took no sides. In order to prevent anyone from grabbing it from me, I bundled it with the hand grenade."

We did not find a KMT agent, but the hand grenade made my stomach churn. To avoid getting caught up in the shooting, we left Taiyuan for Shanghai that night. We found no suspicious KMT activity in the troupes in Nanjing and Beijing. At our debriefings, all the groups that were assigned to other places came back and reported the same thing. To use a trendy phrase during that period, there seemed to be some facts, but no evidence.

One thing which became of great interest at the debriefing was the suspicious material obtained from the dossier on Mo Feixian. In 1950, a KMT agent was parachuted into Guangzhou, only to be captured by the local police, the public security bureau. This agent confessed under interrogation that he came to Guangzhou to meet up with Mo Feixian, who had assisted his mission. Mo, not knowing he was the target of an investigation, went across the border to Hong Kong to perform, which increased suspicion. The public security bureau cast a longer line to capture a larger fish, setting up a fake "escape" for the captured agent to see who he would then meet.

This "runaway" agent was cunning and also very cautious. He stayed put and did nothing for a long time, nor did he contact anyone. As time went by, he was able to escape the surveillance. In China, there was a system of household registration called the "hukou." Local communities were governed by neighborhood committees, which were close to the nearest police post. All citizens were very vigilant and non-residents were spotted without difficulty. A newcomer such as the "runaway" agent, without legal status, could not be registered in a hukou, nor could he find a job, so he would not have money to survive for long. As a result, in 1965, the agent was caught thieving inside the Dongdan Foreign Bookstore in Beijing.

It was on a rehabilitation farm in the high mountains of the far northwest that our troupe members questioned this KMT agent about his relationship with Mo Feixian.

He replied: "Mo Feixian was not on the contact list for my trip to the mainland."

"When you were arrested, why did you confess Mo Feixian was your contact? How did you know his name?"

"When I was being chased, I ran past a theater, and I saw the magician's name on the advertisement board. I memorized it just in case. And I was able to use it during the interrogation."

If this was true, what kind of joke had Heaven played on Mo Feixian! Due to this KMT agent's false information, Mo Feixian had been subjected to constant surveillance, barred from performing overseas, and interned in the cowshed. Even worse, by the time Mo had been cleared of guilt, the Cultural Revolution had started and he was again being investigated.

Mo could not tolerate the torture, and in the summer of 1968 he decided to take his life. He went to the toilet and used a smuggled pair of scissors to cut his throat. Someone in another toilet heard blood pouring into the bowl, and jumped the partition into Mo's cubicle. Mo was taken to a public hospital on Yan'an Road by ambulance. That day, when I came back from a swim, someone told me about Mo's suicide attempt, and I went to visit him in the hospital. I found him with a steel tube inserted in his throat and his blood-stained hands tied to the bed to prevent him attempting to commit suicide again when he recovered from the anesthetic. Mo survived, but his vocal cords had been severely damaged, and he was permanently disabled. Mo's case was not an isolated one; many people in the arts world committed suicide during the Cultural Revolution.

In the 1980s, when China started to institute its reform and opening up policy, Director Wang resumed his post at the troupe. He and Mo, who had both been imprisoned during the Cultural Revolution, had settled their differences. A celebration was organized to honor Mo's forty years of performance. Those who had labeled him a counter-revolutionary academic, and those who had "struggled" him, stood up and praised his achievements. With the political winds changing, everyone was running for cover. Mo himself seemed to have "forgotten" what drove him to his suicide attempt, and voiced his gratitude for the support he had received. Remembering the Cultural Revolution as I sat in the audience, I felt sick in my heart.

. . .

Breaking up pig manure and being conscripted into the special investigation team had failed to "rehabilitate" me. I was determined to do something, in secret, to protect the arts. I did not want to have my artistic life terminated. The idea came to me of making a plaster model of my arm.

It happened this way. One day, a man named Hong Yi was hanging around the troupe. He came from a company that made art products. He pointed at the muscles on my arms and said, "Those muscles are so strong. It would be a great pity if they were not reproduced in plaster." After a pause, he added, "A plaster model of your arm would definitely look great."

Hong Yi gave me some instructions. Intrigued, I got some plaster powder from the props department, but could not find the proper lubricant to oil my arm before applying the plaster. I had to make do with diesel fuel from the metals department. I also needed a place to mix the powder, and chose the stone table next to the metals department. Hong Yi applied the diesel to my arm and added water to the plaster powder, then applied the mixture to my arm. I felt a burning heat on my skin. After the plaster mixture had cooled down, he took the mold off my arm and poured a new mixture into the mold. When I came back from cleaning my diesel-smeared arm, Hong Yi had already smashed the mold and got the model out. He held it up, looked at it appreciatively, and said, "Not bad."

I admired both his artwork and my arm. It became a symbol for me. Whenever I see this arm, I think of the Cultural Revolution and the waste of my youthful years in cruel struggles.

I had other means of silent defiance. I followed a slogan from *Xiang River Commentary,* the student newspaper edited by Mao Zedong: "Savage the physique, and civilize the spirit." I kept following my dream and trained and studied in private. I found a collection of books in a friend's parents' house which had survived the raids of the Four Olds movement. I also found some books taken from raided homes and stored in the troupe's warehouse. Seeing all these books piled up and not being read, I felt it would be a great pity if I did not "borrow" some. Still, I could not read them freely. If I were found reading them, I would certainly become a target of the revolution.

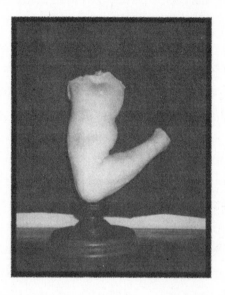

The Arm, 1968: I just wanted to leave something for the future.

I already felt I was under constant suspicion. During the Cultural Revolution, "having connections overseas" was a crime, and many people with any link to the outside world were punished. The scale of the movement made it look like China was back-pedalling to the sea-ban period of the Ming and Qing dynasties, when no one was allowed to undertake maritime activities. This policy had ultimately softened up China for invasion by imperialist countries. In the Chinese translation of *The Communist Manifesto*, I found the following: "The discovery of America, the rounding of the Cape, opened up fresh ground for the rising bourgeoisie. The East Indian and Chinese markets, the colonization of America, trade with the colonies, the increase in the means of exchange and in commodities generally, gave to commerce, to navigation, to industry, an impulse never before known, and thereby, to the revolutionary element in the tottering feudal society, a rapid development." Through this new policy of isolation, was China going to repeat its own unfortunate history?

I refused to believe the ban on overseas connections would last. It was suicidal. I also believed China would sooner or later open its doors and we would perform overseas again. Because of this, learning a foreign language occurred to me, but sadly, the Cultural Revolution had totally destroyed China's education system. All classes were suspended, teachers were cruelly "struggled," and textbooks were destroyed. The desire to learn a foreign language lingered in my mind, unrequited. And my past travels would eventually get me in trouble for "having connections overseas."

* * *

In the summer of 1968, workers' and soldiers' propaganda teams were founded to promote Maoism. A strategic deployment by Mao, this signified the beginning of the end of his use of the radicals. With the sounds of gongs, our acrobatic troupe welcomed the workers' and soldiers' propaganda teams. The soldiers' team consisted of one instructor, one commander and two soldiers from the Fourth Air Force Battalion in Shanghai. The workers' team came from the Shanghai Heavy Machinery Plant. Back in 1964, the Shanghai Party Committee had sent "Four-clear" work teams, comprising its cultural personnel, to this plant to implement the Four Cleanups

Movement, the precursor to the Cultural Revolution. Four years later, the same plant was sending a workers' propaganda team to the cultural system's acrobatic troupe to "lead" a movement. So went the cycle of mutual persecution.

Gong, the instructor from the soldiers' propaganda team, an older man with a dark complexion, a loud voice and a constant simmer of aggression, said at the welcoming assembly, "The presence of the army in the superstructure is intended to transform you bourgeois intellectuals; to struggle mercilessly against all of your non-proletarian thoughts."

The workers' representative, a man in his forties, then spoke. "The presence of our workers' class in the superstructure is to mind your heads and your feet. Even though we workers may not be educated, we know best the thoughts of Mao Zedong. The works written by our beloved Chairman Mao were written for us, the working class, and the poor and lower-middle class peasants. Hence, we are the best candidates to propagate Mao Zedong's Thought."

The propaganda teams were proud of not having any culture or knowledge. People inside the arts world were changing, too. Those in the singing theater badmouthed the performing theater, calling them "a bunch of whores," while the performers said the same of the singers. The people in the writers' association took pride in carrying a pen as a fashion statement. Everything went upside down, and civilization was turned back to savage times.

The Communist Party is renowned for its numerous meetings. I have forgotten how many meetings I attended, and each time my mind would wander. That was the case when I sat in the audience of this welcoming assembly. I was not sure I understood what the workers' representative was saying. My big question was how a bunch of proud illiterates could propagate the glorious Mao Zedong's thoughts.

I had studied Mao Zedong's works, but still found myself in a state of confusion. I envied those workers who had got rid of their "immovable" status and been empowered by their working-class credibility and enlightened in such a special way.

The propaganda teams took over from the radicals who had been in charge, forcing them to hand over the seal they had recently acquired. The radical leaders were ordered to write confessions about each and every matter in which they had participated, including those formerly known as "revolutionary," which were now called "assaulting," "smashing" and "looting." At the beginning of the Cultural Revolution, the radicals in our troupe had raided the Cultural Bureau files, using physical force to get their way. These self-declared brave revolutionary fighters realized they had been manipulated, and were now to be swept away as historical rubbish.

* * *

My old acrobatics teacher Li Dianqi was an honest person who always avoided trouble and had no enemies. Ever since liberation, he had slid under the constantly changing political movements. He had not been affected in the early days of the Cultural Revolution, and thought he could keep it that way. But Li had a terribly dangerous secret. One day, he came to me with a stern face and said discreetly, "Come to my house on Sunday. I've got something to discuss with you."

I could tell from his expression that it was something important. As he was my teacher, I treated him as a father. I would do anything for him. This is a Chinese tradition. That Sunday afternoon, I went to his house. Li had sent his wife and children to the cinema, so we were alone. He started talking in an agitated voice.

"I asked you to come today to discuss a very awkward matter."

He handed me a two-page English identification certificate on which was a passport photo of him in his youth, and also his signature in English.

"Let me explain this identification certificate." He inhaled hard on his cigarette, and said: "In 1941, my brothers and I went on a performance tour of the United States. While we were waiting for our ship in Hong Kong, the Japanese launched the Pacific War, and then occupied Hong Kong. Since America and Japan were at war, there were no more ships sailing from Hong Kong to the United States, so we had to go back to China. When we arrived in Guilin in Guangxi Province, we met Tian Han, who wrote the lyrics for 'The March of the Volunteers' (the national anthem of the People's Republic of China) and was a member of the Communist Party. He said we should go to Yan'an. Yan'an was a very poor place, and we decided not to go. Instead, we went to Yunnan Province."

During the anti-Japanese war, Li Dianqi had worked with our US allies on the air base in Yunnan Province. Having learned English while performing overseas with acrobatic troupes, he was useful in the fight against the Japanese. But after the People's Republic of China was founded, the relationship between China and America turned sour and, when wars broke out on our doorstep in Korea and Vietnam, the United States became the chief enemy of China. Li had been suffering huge stress, worrying day and night that his military service at the US air base would be discovered, and bring ruin to him and his family.

"Looking back, I used to wish I had gone to Yan'an," he told me. "If I had followed Tian Han's suggestion, I would have become a chief, or a section leader of a bureau. But now that we are involved in this Cultural Revolution, seeing those cadres struggled in those sessions, their families destroyed, I feel it was lucky that I did not choose to go to Yan'an then. Otherwise, I would be just like those cadres."

He did not tell me the specific nature of his work at the US air base, and I knew it was in my best interest to know as little as possible.

"What you are now holding in your hands is my identification certificate from that period," he said. "The investigation into people who have connections overseas is now being tightened up. If those propaganda teams came to know about this, it would be disastrous. Please help me find a way. What should I do?"

Teacher Li was asking for my help! If he were to be investigated, could he handle the physical and mental torture? What would happen to his wife, and his children, who were still at school? I could not even guess. There was no way out other than to destroy the certificate. If any investigation did come up, the result could only be that "there may be a fact, but there is no evidence."

"Have you told anyone this, including the troupe leaders, your wife and others in the troupe?" I asked him.

"No. I have told no one."

"That's good."

"What should I do?" he asked eagerly.

"Burn it. Without evidence, no one can do anything about it."

He thought for a moment, and said, "Good!"

I took a match from the box on the table and said, "Let me burn it for you."

Upon his nod, I lit the match, burned the certificate and threw it in the ashtray. I flushed the ashes down the toilet. There it went, a piece of evidence from the anti-Japanese war, vanishing to the noise of flushing water and Li's sigh.

*　*　*

In 1969, the Ninth National Congress of the Chinese Communist Party took place, a monumental event in the political lives of the Chinese people. Mao Zedong's message, broadcast to the public on the radio after the congress, was that "this Cultural Revolution is absolutely necessary."

One of the important tasks for the ninth congress was to write into the constitution of the Chinese Communist Party that, since Liu Shaoqi had been purged, Lin Biao was the successor and closest comrade-in-arms of Mao Zedong. When the workers' and soldiers' propaganda teams reported this to us, Instructor Gong provided some juicy details. Unlike previous congresses, Chairman Mao had sat at the center, in between two factions. To his left were leftists, like his wife Jiang Qing, Kang Sheng, Chen Boda, Zhang Chunqiao and Yao Wenyuan; to his right were the rightists, such as Zhu De and Chen Yi as well as "the broken-fingered old man, Ye Jianying," as Gong called the revered general, who had reputedly banged the table so hard when arguing with leftists at Huairen Hall that he fractured a finger. I was shocked to hear a grassroots leader verbally abusing the leader of the army. So much for what Deputy Chairman Lin had said in a documentary broadcast: "This is a congress of unity, a congress of victory."

The congress also determined that a lot of professional talent in scientific research, the arts and sport must be sent to the countryside for the "rehabilitation of their minds through hard work." Once again, I was sent out to the country.

My agricultural labor stint in 1969 was different from the previous times, as I was told to prepare for a long stay, though of course I wasn't told exactly how long. I packed my things, such as my clothing with patches over the patches, and gumboots, mosquito net and blankets, and jumped onto one of the trucks arranged by the Cultural Bureau. I did not even ask where I was going. The location didn't interest me. No matter where it was, I was being sent there to reform my thoughts.

The truck fleet stopped at the foot of Sheshan Hill in Songjiang County. The sun setting over a vacant church on the top of the hill created a serene scene. We set up our camp not far from the picturesque church and started another round of atonement. As a cultural performer, the party had labeled me an intellectual, so I found myself loaded with bourgeois original sin. Only through hard work and political study could I hope to atone.

The work in the paddies was seasonal. We were there for the autumn harvest and our repentance was judged by how quickly we worked. Each morning at around four am we would start, and we would only stop when the moon rose. I, like everyone else, kept my sufferings to myself.

While I was toiling in the field, another thought began to crawl out of my misery: All things in the world have effects on one another. If there is to be a bad thing, there is going to be a good thing, like two sides of a coin. If I could turn physical torture into physical training, of my body and my muscles, I might feel better.

I considered how to turn farm laboring into a form of exercise. In my professional performance, I needed two kinds of strength: stamina and eruptive force. Farm labor required a lot of stamina. How could I make use of the work in the fields to increase my eruptive force? I thought about it over and over. I divided the types of work into several categories, and I paced my effort, sometimes quick and sometimes slow, and built up my eruptive power when I had to do certain things in a short period of time. I began to find this training very helpful and effective.

Fu Cong, the famous pianist, had once said, "The hands meant for pianos should not be used to handle a hoe." But I had to make the best of the situation. I tried different ways of grabbing the sickle and other tools. When I was using a hoe, I paid attention to strengthening the muscles in my arms and shoulders. Walking with weight on one shoulder from a carrying pole, I trained my balance. I also shifted the weight between shoulders so as not to burden one side. Before each day's work, I did warm-up exercises. After a while, I could see improvement in the strength in my shoulders, back and waist, and also in my arms.

Not everyone could handle such heavy work, especially not the old workers from the workers' propaganda team who were overseeing us. Watching them puffing and trying to catch their breath, with their hands on their waists, their legs trembling, I said to myself, Poor old men. They are suffering from the task of transforming our worldview.

Members of the propaganda team were also human beings. They had to put on a protective mask in a dangerous political situation. But once that mask was removed, trouble would ensue and they would turn against each other.

Jiang was one of the young technicians in the factory who now led us in running the farm; he had a scholarly look, and he was not physically strong. One day, soon after daybreak, he guided us to harvest rice. We worked until sunset, but there was still a big area of paddies waiting to be harvested. To speed things up, Jiang announced that whoever finished his allocated lot could have a rest. We all got pumped up, and worked extremely hard to finish. On the way back to our brigade, everyone praised Jiang's "wise" move. But that evening, Jiang was criticized by the leader of the propaganda team, who said he had committed the error of encouraging individualism, and treading the "capitalist" path. Two days later, a long-faced Jiang delivered his "profound" self-criticism to the best of his ability during our political study session.

Jiang's self-criticism confused me even further. Why was efficiency considered to be treading the capitalist path? Did we not need efficiency in socialism? One member of the workers' propaganda team supervising us was a woman named Gui, who had graduated from high school before the Cultural Revolution and started working in a factory. She liked reading classic books, Chinese and foreign ones alike. One night in the dormitory, she chatted with her roommates about her favorite foreign books. The next day, someone reported this to the propaganda team and said Gui was trying to corrupt some of the revolutionary artistic workers. The propaganda team criticized her bourgeois thoughts, saying that she was not fit for the team, and sent her back to her original factory.

There was a pig farm in the brigade, and at the end of the rows of pigsties was a feed barn, No. 12 pig shed, which became a retreat for me and two others, a young man named Liang Tie and a young woman named Su Lan, for the next eight months. They were two or three years younger than me, but we became good friends. Right next to the shed was an open septic tank 3 yards in diameter, giving off a powerful stink. I was not sure if it was because I was adapting or just losing my sense of smell, but after a while in the pig shed I did not notice the stink. Whether that was proof that I had "changed class feelings," I had not the slightest idea.

During those eight months in the countryside, we labored through the two busiest seasons, autumn and spring. In winter, when we were not too busy, we had to undertake endless studies to "make revolution at the deepest core of the soul." Everybody tried to talk in the study sessions about how laboring had transformed their worldview. Everybody also knew that everybody else was lying to impress the propaganda teams.

At the beginning, I had hoped it would rain, so that we would not have to go out and work. I thought I could lie down on the hay and listen to the rain, and let my body recover from the heavy labor. But now, rain was the last thing I hoped for, because when it rained, those of us who had the "original sin" were to sit together and "fight selfishness and repudiate revisionism."

At study sessions, members of the propaganda team would sometimes take the lead. One spoke about his observations. The people lived along a river. This member found out that he was near the lower part, and that people living upstream cleaned their chamber pots in the river. He did not feel good about it at the beginning, but he thought about it again and convinced himself that the people in the village had been doing this for many, many generations, so it was he himself who must change his mental discrimination against the rural people. "I am grateful for this opportunity to come and work in the countryside," he said, concluding his talk about the benefits of bathing in farmers' effluent.

Everybody followed suit and talked about how they had changed their worldview. I remembered a story I had known since I was little. A father, seeing his son always had a runny nose, told him, "Wipe your nose, and I'll buy you candies." The son turned his head and when he faced his father again, his nose was clean.

Then he asked his father for candies, and his father responded, "You fool."

The son let go of the control on his nose, and it began to run again. He also said, "You fool."

That was how I felt about our political sessions. Everyone was trying to fool each other. I hated this kind of spiritual torture. In order to protect the purity of my heart, I did not want to talk about my real thoughts. I tried to stay silent and only talked when my name was called. When that happened, I would retell stories I'd heard, changing just the names. I was unashamed of this. I was like everyone else, putting on a mask, protecting myself.

With the coming of winter, the sour odors lingering above the pig shed diminished. The annoying flies, and the mosquitoes which were my enemies at night, had disappeared. Snowflakes danced in the sky. Cold winds rushed across the fields, through the crevices in the bamboo walls of our shed. Out of the frying pan, into the . . . freezer? We felt we would die from the cold at night. I dreamed I was with a group called the Russian December Gang, and we were being exiled to frozen Siberia. We were walking with great difficulty on the snow and ice. One of us fell, and I reached out to help him, but I tumbled after him into a freezing hole. Then I woke up. I looked at my thin blanket peppered with snowflakes, and felt a terrible chill.

Somehow, the privation stimulated my will to fight back. I thought to myself, "If I can't even handle the cold, then what else can I say about my ideals, my career and my success?" I talked to my two friends, Liang Tie and Su Lan, and we decided to take up the challenge and strengthen our will. We would get up at five in the morning, when it was still pitch-dark, and break some ice on the surface of the river to use as water to brush our teeth and wash our faces. Our hands and faces turned red from the cold water. After that, we went back to our room, removed our cotton-padded coats and started our exercises. My frozen fingers would hardly support me in my handstand, while my frozen toes would not even allow me to stand on my feet for long. We were still young, however, and the vitality inside us had been sparked. We knew that to challenge ourselves was the first step to challenging anything else. We promised to exercise like this each morning. No one was to miss a day, even if injured.

To "suffer the pains others could not endure" was quintessential in the training of talent in China, and I had been through this regime from a very young age. When I look back at those years of hardship, I comprehend the meaning of the old saying "A man must have some spirit." Many years later, when he became a famous magician, Liang Tie told me, "During that period, when we exercised each morning, that strengthened my willpower, and had a great effect upon my path in life." Su Lan also did well on the stage, performing the one-arm handstand with spinning plates. She recalled, "Despite the cold, I felt happiest during those two hours of each day."

The attitude of the poor farmers changed with the season. When we were busy harvesting, they were kind to us. After the harvest, when there was nothing to do, a coldness appeared in their faces. Our presence was no longer welcomed, as we occupied some of their space. The propaganda team submitted their request for our return, and we went back to Shanghai at the end of 1969.

13

BEHIND BARS

In 1970, I was twenty-three. On the morning of February 28, while walking in the courtyard in the troupe compound, I had a strange feeling. Wherever I went, I saw Shang, a soldier from the soldiers' propaganda team, following me at a distance. Suddenly, he walked straight up to me and said, "Follow me to the team office."

Not knowing what was happening, I followed him cautiously to the office, which was located in the storeroom where devices for magical performances were kept. It was a highly secret room. When I went in, I saw Instructor Gong and Battalion Chief Li sitting there.

Gong said in a very stern voice, "Do you know why you have been called here?"

"I don't know," I replied, totally confused.

"You don't know your own problem? You must confess everything you had to do with the May 16 counter-revolutionary activities," Gong said, referring to a supposed conspiracy named after a Communist Party document released on May 16, 1966.

"Me?"

"Who else? We never wrong a good man and will never let a bad one go. We have evidence of you conducting anti-revolutionary activities, and that's why we have brought you here. You should know our party policy without us telling you, right? Confession leads to leniency, while resistance leads to severity. You make your choice. We have plenty of time to figure out your problems. Now I announce the beginning of your personal study group on Mao Zedong Thought."

Millions were investigated like this during the Cultural Revolution. But it had never crossed my mind that someone like me would become a target for segregation and investigation. No matter how much hardship I was facing, I always thought about glorifying our country. I looked at them, dumbfounded.

Li saw this, and issued his order wearily: "Shang, watch him closely. Follow him to his dorm and collect his belongings, and send him to the segregation room."

To prevent me from destroying any possible evidence, Shang checked my packed belongings very carefully and said, "Follow me."

The segregation room was a shower room in the quiet corner of the courtyard. In winter, there was no hot water supply, so the shower room was not in use. It was a place to store clothing, and it had no windows, making escape impossible under the eyes of a guard. They certainly knew how to make good use of existing facilities.

"Get in!" Shang pointed at the door.

Walking through the passageway outside the shower room, I saw Pu, an electrician who had become a guard, smirking nastily at me. They were putting a 24-hour watch on me in three shifts. In one hand I carried my belongings and bed sheets; with the other I pushed open the door to the room where I was to participate in my personal study group on Mao Zedong Thought.

The wall in the shower room was thirty feet long by 13 feet wide. On it was printed the slogan "Confession leads to leniency, while resistance leads to severity." A wooden plank bed was in the corner.

There was only a 25-watt light bulb. In this room without a window, and full of damp air, I rugged myself up in a coat, and I was restless even when sitting. I could not understand why I had lost my freedom. Meals were provided each day, and I was followed when I went to the toilet. I had absolutely no contact with anyone, and was not even allowed to talk to the guards.

For three days, I was not interrogated at all. This was a very effective method to crush people under investigation. Alone, with nothing happening, a prisoner would begin to feel huge pressure, panic, and then be unable to control him or herself. During these three days, however, I pondered very hard on why I would be considered an anti-revolutionary. I could not find a reason, even after going over and over all that I had said and done in the past few years. I came to this conclusion: I firmly believe that I am not an anti-revolutionary. I am innocent.

But the propaganda teams were always "correct" by definition. Who would believe a prisoner, who was guilty by definition? I still vividly remembered a book I had read called *The Stalin Era*. The author, Anna Louise Strong, used irrefutable evidence to reveal how Stalin gave the Cheka, the Soviet secret police, powers beyond the parameters of the Soviet constitution to arrest innocent people, and to broaden the scope of their purges to his political enemies. China was going through its own era of violent extra-legal purges. It was worse for others, of course. For example, that same year, at a public trial in the People's Square, a performer at the cultural stadium was accused of not imitating well enough the ballet dances created by Chairman Mao's wife, Jiang Qing. Accused of denigrating the revolutionary model dramas, he was executed by firing squad.

My three days of waiting were torturous. Each day seemed to be longer than the one before. The cold west wind blew outside, but the inside of the shower room was no warmer. The coldness went all the way into my heart, crushing my will. I now had frostbite, which I had never had before. I wrapped myself in my coat and curled up in bed.

On the fourth day, Shang pushed open the door.

"Come."

It was time for questioning. Full of uncertainty, I entered the soldiers' propaganda team office for the second time. Gong was in charge. Mine had to be a serious case for him to be supervising it personally.

Without preamble, he said: "You have been given three days. Have you thought through the problems you want to confess?"

I told him the truth. "I have thought about this for three days, and I really don't know what it is you want me to confess to. I didn't participate in any May 16 organization."

"You are playing dumb with me. You don't know your own problems? We know what you have done, and that's why we have segregated you. I am warning you once more. Confess, as confession leads to leniency, while resistance leads to severity. Which way you want to go depends on you."

I could neither defend myself nor figure out what I was supposed to confess. I knew that the more I made up confessions, the more problems I would create, and the more they could accuse me of. I was not going to manufacture any evidence against myself, so I chose to remain silent.

Gong said, "Well, well, well. You are not going to cry unless you see your coffin, right? Let me give you a hint. Have you recently seen someone from Beijing, a Red Guard advocate?"

Then I knew.

"Are you talking about Peng Xiaomeng?"

"Right, you must confess your relationship with her and her family, those people from the old Shanghai City Committee and the

East China Bureau. You must confess all anti-Cultural Revolution speech and behavior, yours and theirs."

Mao's initial reception of Peng Xiaomeng and the Red Guard on August 18, 1966, on the rostrum in Tiananmen Square.

I had met Peng Xiaomeng back in 1959 after a performance in Beijing while we were getting ready to go to Africa. Peng's elder brother, Xiao Yan, had been the artistic director and music conductor of our African trip, and their father was secretary-general of the Chinese Red Cross. Peng was a smiling, confident girl with glasses and a long braided ponytail. I knew for certain that Peng was not an anti-revolutionary. But the Cultural Revolution had reinterpreted those innocent days. She had been mentioned in a letter Mao had written in the early days of the Cultural Revolution to Tsinghua University High School, and was considered ideologically suspect for that reason. Their agenda became clear to me. They wanted to smash not only the major leaders from the central ministries and the city committee, but they also wanted to purge their children.

The Chinese Red Cross was a government ministry. Totally shocked, I looked at Gong in amazement.

"Don't look at me like that. I've got even more surprises to tell you. You go on and write your confession about the relationship between you and Peng, and her anti-revolutionary clique, including the overall nature of your activities, tasks and the hidden hand behind the scenes. Here is some paper for you. Go back to the shower room and write it up."

Gong then waved to Shang to take me back. When I returned to the shower room, a table and chair had been brought in. I put the paper on the table. I blew onto my frostbitten hands and started to rub them together. I paced up and down, in order to generate some body heat. Peng and others must also have been arrested. But on what grounds? I didn't know. At least it was now clear why I was in here.

I had to write something. But no matter how serious the situation was, no matter whether they believed me or not, I would not write anything that would incriminate me. I would write what I knew, irrespective of the consequences. Holding a pen in my frozen fingers, I started.

At the end of 1959, when we were in Beijing preparing for our visit to Africa, on Sundays we young performers had nowhere to go. So, Xiao Yan, the artistic director and conductor of the orchestra for the African trip, took us to his father's house for a visit. His father was the secretary-general of the China Red Cross. It was there I met Xiao Yan's younger brother and his younger sister Peng Xiaomeng.

After coming back from the African trip, we went to Xiao's house again. At the dinner table, Xiao's father pointed at one of the dishes and told him, 'This lion's head meatball casserole was cooked using up all the meat coupons we've saved for the past few months. The vegetables on the table are all grown in our own backyard. You've been away for a few months, and you wouldn't have known our country is now in a very difficult situation.'

On International Labor Day, May 1, 1963, we went and performed on the Tiananmen rostrum, and Xiao Yan's father was also in the audience. After seeing me performing, standing on my hands, he came over and took me back to the table where he was sitting, a table for the Health Ministry and for the Red Cross. He said to them, 'A little friend of our family.'

In 1966, when the Vietnamese Acrobatic Troupe was visiting Shanghai, we accompanied them to watch a news documentary in the little hall at the Jin Jiang Hotel. The documentary was of a reception held during Mao's visit with the Red Guards on August 18. I saw Peng speaking on the Tiananmen rostrum, and was surprised to learn that, virtually overnight, she had become an important figure in the Cultural Revolution. In October that same year, she came to Shanghai on the 'Nationwide Linkup' and she gave me two photos. One was a photo of her being received alone by Mao, and the other was of her and other Red Guards with Mao.

I talked to Peng, and talked a lot, but not about political issues. Because she was the daughter of a leader, and I was a normal citizen, we belonged to different social groups. Her political views were aggressive, and mine conservative, so we didn't talk about politics since we had no common ground, but that didn't prevent us from being friends.

Due to my lack of political awareness, whenever we met I didn't ever observe her and analyze her from the perspective of the Class Struggle. After this incident, I have come to realize my mistake. In the future, I will try my best to raise the bar in the sense of Class Struggle.

Satisfied with the formulaic language of my confession, I signed and handed it to the guard. Two days later, I was taken away for another interrogation.

As soon as I walked in, Gong's livid face told me he was not satisfied with my confession. He was in fact very dissatisfied. He banged the papers on the table, and yelled at me: "This is what you have written? Do you think I am a three-year-old? Who are you trying to deceive? Go back and write it again. You 'had no common ground,' but you could still be good friends? In a society where classes exist, there are only people divided by classes, and there are no friendships outside your class. Can there be friendship between the landlords and the peasants? You must do as Comrade Jiang Qing said. The ugly daughter-in-law must see the parents-in-law sooner or later. You must confess your issues like pouring out beans from a bucket. Peng Xiaomeng's father is an old anti-revolutionary who was against Comrade Jiang Qing, and he has been arrested. Birds of a feather flock together. Such are the people you messed around with! Do you now understand your issue?"

Peng's father was an anti-revolutionary? When he was involved in the revolution, Gong was still in nappies. Without Peng's father and his comrades, how could Gong have what he had now?

"What? What are you thinking about?" Gong interrupted my thoughts.

"I am thinking about how I could better confess my problems," I responded.

"Not better! You must fully confess everything you know about

Peng and her friends, and also your venomous attacks on the head-quarters of the proletarian workers!"

A lot of secrets were spread among the children of those leaders. Peng had told me some "not-to-be-proliferated" secrets. In order to confuse him, I told some of the secrets that he should not know.

"In the '30s, when Jiang Qing was still an actress in Shanghai, she went to Yan'an, vowing to marry the number one man in the world, and she became Madame Mao. At gatherings Jiang Qing would tell the masses that she was greeting them on behalf of Chairman Mao. However, Mao had said, 'She is she, and I am I. She cannot represent me.'"

Gong's initial shock was overtaken by anger.

"That's bullshit. Comrade Jiang Qing is the wife of our great leader, Chairman Mao, the chief officer of the Central Cultural Revolution Group. Chairman Mao would never say anything like that. This is total blasphemy! You are lying about the relationship between the chiefs in the proletariat headquarters. I am now warn-ing you, all you have said stops here in this office. You must not tell any of this to anyone else. Otherwise, you will suffer severe conse-quences. Besides, now that you've shown that Peng spoke adversely about Jiang Qing, you must also have witnessed many other serious anti-revolutionary deeds and speeches that you haven't disclosed yet. Confess them one by one, including your own."

What did I have to confess? I thought hard again. This was a time in history when anything could have a new meaning, depend-ing on one's perspective. There was no such thing as truth. I didn't know what to say, or what not to say in order to save myself.

After thinking for a while, I said, "During my talks with Peng, I mentioned that in 1962, I saw Wang Guangmei, Chairman Liu Shaoqi's wife, wearing an elegant qipao dress, and she looked beautiful when receiving the wives of the heads of state from Africa. I said Wang accompanied the foreign guests and appeared on the stage. Wang was kind and left a good impression with me."

"You are singing the praises of the biggest capitalist roaders in the Communist Party in China!" Gong raised his voice. "Of China's Khrushchev's dirty wife—Wang Guangmei! You are just trying to paint things in a good light. You are the socialist foundation of such capitalist roaders in the party who are trying to restore capitalism. How dare you reserve your opinion? Making a thorough confession is the only way out for you!"

After more than twenty days and several more interrogation sessions, I gradually became calmer. I was no longer as afraid or confused as I had been at the beginning. Their interrogations revealed that they did not have any evidence of me participating in the May 16 anti-revolutionary organization. Otherwise, they would have shown it to me. Actually, they could not have had any, as I had never done anything like that.

From my experience with the special investigation team, I guessed that they might have heard my name mentioned during their investigation of Peng. They thought it worth doing a check on me. Now I had to keep my mouth shut; I would suffer severely if I confessed to anything I did not do. I would stick to that no matter what. I did not dare dream that they would find me innocent, but I became immune to my earlier anxiety when I had no idea what I was being accused of.

Being an orphan, I had always felt that I wasn't loved. After this segregation, I felt somehow lucky that I didn't have any relatives, as nobody would be out there suffering from worry for me. If that was a blessing, I suppose it was wearing a very good disguise.

✦ ✶ ✱

Spring came, which meant more agricultural activities for idle intellectuals. Meanwhile, I was the only one still rugged up in a big coat, living in the cold shower room. I was brought into a hall where the propaganda teams had called a meeting to boost morale for troupe members going out for further re-education by farmers. After announcing plans for the farm work, Gong suddenly said, "When in the rural area, you must not forget class struggle, and the class struggle in our troupe is still a serious matter. For example, one of our members is learning a foreign language. Is this not treason? That person is Xue Jingjing. His problem is not a simple one, but a very serious one. We must investigate and find out all about him."

A wave of whispers spread through the audience. Believe it or not, there were troupe members who wondered if I was actually studying a foreign language. When they left for the countryside, I was transferred to the Shanghai Acrobatic Theatre, near Shanghai Library. The ground had been abandoned since the beginning of the Cultural Revolution. Instead of acrobatics, it now staged class struggle sessions.

On the day of my transfer, I packed my belongings. When I walked out, the bright sunlight made me dizzy. I closed my eyes and waited a long while before I could open them and view the wonderful spring. How lovely was the sun! Even prisoners had yard time in the sun, but not me.

My new segregation room, about 20 square feet, was next to a tiger cage. I had a bed, a table and a chair. The only window was blocked, and the door, of course, was locked. Surrounding the room were animal training fields enclosed by iron bars. What a good place to lock someone up. Each night after midnight, I would be woken up

Shanghai, 1970: The animal training area of the Shanghai Acrobatic Theatre, where I was detained.

by a torch-bearing guard checking on me. After that, it was difficult to get back to sleep. I still had to cope with interrogations now and then, but they were not as severe or frequent. The propaganda team seemed to be waiting for something.

I had heard that if a person is kept in solitude for too long, he might lose his sanity. I didn't believe that at first, but after three months in isolation, I started to understand. One day, I was taken in a bus to a public struggle session in Xinzhuang. Looking out of the bus window, I saw the buildings rushing toward me. I saw pedestrians in panic in the streets and laneways. Broken strips of big-character posters flew everywhere, like white skeletons swirling in the wind. I heard nothing at all. *Is this a ghost town?* I wondered. *Why am I here? I am still young, and I shouldn't be here.* A voice from afar said, "Do you think there is any age limit on the road to death?"

Before I could respond, the bus came to an abrupt halt. My body jolted forward and then backward. The ghost town disappeared.

I heard people in the bus yelling at the driver, "You stupid idiot, don't you know how to drive?"

The driver leaned out of the window and scolded a bike rider: "You looking for death? Find another place!"

I realized I had been hallucinating, the result of stress and being so long in solitude.

Coming back from Xinzhuang, I told myself that when, one day, I got out of confinement, I would still be strong in mind and body, and my brain would still be lucid. I must not be a lamb waiting to be slaughtered. I would not waste my time even in the segregation room. The first thing I needed to do each morning was exercise my vocal cords with a few light roars, trying not to be heard by the guards. I just wanted to see if my vocal cords had atrophied. Then I would try some stretches.

The surprising fact is, if one overcomes the darkness in one's heart, all one will be able to see is brightness and hope. The surrounding world will no longer be that bad, and the force of life will have become more powerful in the fight against fate.

While performing in Chongqing in 1964, we had visited Zhazi Cave Prison. We were told that Communist Party revolutionaries detained there by the KMT were allowed access to books and publications that were not forbidden by the government. In order to better contribute to the cause of the Communist Party, those detainees kept studying all sorts of subjects, including philosophy, Russian and natural science. We were also told that the martyrs kept their revolutionary ideals alive in their minds, and retained their strong will. They read the newspapers published by the KMT government and decided that the truth was the opposite of what had been written. But I was only a commoner, and was not allowed to read anything apart from the selected works of Mao Zedong. Not a single newspaper, or any magazines, let alone any other kinds of books.

The lesson I remembered from the caves at Chongqing was that a prison is, to a revolutionary, a special school.

I had a lot of time in the segregation room to think about some serious issues. The proletariat class was supposed to quash its class enemies. Why had a lot of working-class people, including me, been the target of their persecution? Were there no human rights in this republic? The party had told us we were the people who had been emancipated; we were the owners of the country. But why didn't the owners of the country feel safe? Why was the persecution of innocents so common in China, and why was everyone tolerating it?

The opportunity to study and learn while in a bad situation is rare in life, even a treasure. I still had my dreams and the freedom of my thoughts. At night, when all was quiet, I would think about how I could achieve and surpass the performance of Ocinsky, a Russian

Chongqing, 1964: Outside the high walls of Zhazi Cave Prison. One could easily feel the oppressive atmosphere.

acrobat who had lost an arm in the Second World War. He was still able to achieve miracles in the acrobatic world. I saw him in a movie about the Great Moscow Circus in the 1960s in Shanghai. With Russian classical music in the background, Ocinsky was standing on a pole on a revolving platform onstage. A spotlight from the bottom of the pole made the audience see only the silhouette of Ocinsky, with his single arm, doing a handstand like a beautiful Italian sculpture. To me, that was the pinnacle of acrobatic skill, and when I pictured it in the segregation room, I was a free man.

As an acrobat, my first ambition had been to surpass Lauzik Malgit's handstand, a demonstration of force. My second was to replicate Ocinsky's handstand on a revolving platform. In the segregation room, thinking about achieving these summits of performance, I was like a seed hidden under a big rock. Through a crack in the rock, the seed can germinate and grow. My passion for my career was my life, and I felt it all the time. This passion would not be crushed by political elements.

Since I had plenty of time, I was able to conduct a thorough comparison between Ocinsky and myself. Age: He was past his career peak, while I was still young. Body shape: He had great flexibility and a good figure, but lacked force and strength. I had great strength, and could perform tasks of great difficulty, yet I needed to improve my flexibility. He had only one arm. I had two, which meant I could do not only his one-arm handstand, but also a two-arm handstand. He had conquered the unstable equilibrium in a spinning motion, but I hadn't started yet. As for will, mine was as strong as his. After this comparison, I realized that it would not be impossible to surpass Ocinsky.

If I could go out and do some work, and stretch my legs and breathe the fresh air, that would be great. But I had only one opportunity, after a struggle session. The cleaners were short of staff and they asked me to do some sweeping. While I was sweeping the floor industriously, one of my former classmates came close and asked me in a low voice, "How do you feel in there?"

Before I was able to answer, the smirking electrician-guard Pu saw us and sent me back inside, denying me even the precious chance to sweep a floor.

The weather gradually warmed up. I had company, a fly, which had flown through the crack in the door. Back in 1958, there had been a campaign to eliminate the Four Pests: mosquitoes, rats, flies and sparrows. All around China, people were crazy about it, and we even had to produce a show to dramatize and promote the need for the movement. We prepared a live drama in the street, and I was the fly. Now I was sharing a cell with one.

On the one hand, the fly was annoying, buzzing around all the time, and potentially bringing in germs. On the other hand, I realized that a fly was also a life. Even though it might be annoying, this fly would be company; it would give me something to be interested in, and it would reduce the boredom. Watching the fly, I found its behavior different from what I had been taught in the past about flies, that they gravitate to smelly things and delicious food. It was my observation that the fly had a diversity of interests. Why else would it be here with me? Also, it didn't stay in the dark corners. It liked the light, and often landed on the windowpane, where sunshine could come through. It just went after something it liked at any given moment.

Reflecting on myself, and the people around me, I came to understand that people, when faced with unpredictable political movements, are like a bunch of blind flies bumping into each other. We all believed we were searching for a better life. Thank you, little fly, for enlightening me on this simple yet hard to comprehend truth.

. . .

Prior to my release on July 28, five months after I was detained, a denunciation meeting was held against me in Xinzhuang. Before a case could be closed, this routine procedure had to be carried out, otherwise they could not justify the unlawful detention. Instructor Gong and Battalion Chief Li were sitting on the stage. Before the stage were the troupe members. They were relaxed: this meeting got them out of half a day's hard labor in the fields. They were used to class struggle meetings, and had become inured to the ups and downs of political movements.

After the crowd had sung the "Internationale" and "The East Is Red," and chanted slogans from Mao's works and other slogans reinforcing unity, the crier shouted, "Bring up Xue Jingjing!"

I was pushed onto the stage, and stood in one corner with my head down. I heard several accusations read aloud from prepared scripts. To my surprise, nothing was mentioned about the May 16 charges, nor the foreign language study. Instead, I was accused of reading booklets written by Marx and Lu Xun, which they found when searching my belongings.

The person who read out the allegations quoted Deputy Chairman Lin Biao: "Among the classical works of Marxism and Leninism, we must put 99 percent of our efforts into the study of Chairman Mao's words. They are the textbooks for revolution."

Then he pointed at me and said, "Why did you go against Lin's words and read the books of Marx? Deputy Chairman Lin has said Chairman Mao's words are of the highest standard and authority, and contain ultimate power. Each of his sentences is the truth. One is equivalent to ten thousand sentences. You didn't study Chairman Mao's works, and went to study those hard-to-chew words of Marx which were written over one hundred years ago.

What are you trying to demonstrate? Isn't it a fact that in your studies you abandon what's next to you, and search for what is afar? You are putting the books on Marxism and Mao's Thoughts against each other, and as a result, we can see a problem with your point of view."

In a country which deemed Marxism-Leninism the theoretical foundation of its government, my crime was to read books about Marxism-Leninism. But my accusers looked so serious—was I missing something? I was then accused of reading the works of Lu Xun. My accuser went on to quote Mao: "One must not simply copy Lu Xun's structure in writing essays, but also learn the way he writes. Lu Xun was under the control of the dark forces of the then authorities, and he had no freedom of speech, so he used his pen and his ironic writing style as a weapon to fight." He continued, accusing me of "studying with great interest the hard-to-chew text which reflected darkness in one's heart, yet this is a time full of brightness, the time of Mao Zedong."

Each denunciation was the same, like an amateur chef cooking the same dishes over and over again. I couldn't help but drift away. I pictured Fidel Castro, who, after being arrested, defended himself in court, upholding his belief in violent revolution. His speeches in the trial were later compiled in a book, *History Will Absolve Me*. During the honeymoon period of China and Cuba's formal relationship, this book was translated and published in China. I was not born a rebel, but I really admired Castro for his eloquent speech and his courage in defending himself.

Before they finished the denunciation meeting, I was declared to have committed "serious political errors." I felt deep sadness at not being afforded basic human dignity and justice.

In the truck from Xinzhuang back to Shanghai, the guard told me, "You can move out of the segregation room tonight."

However, by the time we got there it was too late, so I stayed the night, after the guard had left without putting the lock on. That night was extremely quiet. I thought back over the past five months, over the horrible nature of class struggle. In a country where there is no security, one's efforts, including career, marriage and family, are like a sandcastle, and can be washed away in a moment by any political wave.

14

THE TURNING POINT

On March 18, 1970, Cambodian Prime Minister Lon Nol overthrew Prince Norodom Sihanouk, the head of state, who was visiting France. Sihanouk then came to Beijing, and was warmly received by Premier Zhou Enlai at the airport. Between February and March 1971, Sihanouk visited Eastern China, accompanied by Marshal Ye Jianying. To welcome him, the Shanghai Revolutionary Committee organized an arts program, which included a performance by our acrobatic troupe on February 24, 1971.

For five years, the troupe had hardly even practiced. Our costumes had either been destroyed by the Four Olds movement or lost. The troupe was not well equipped in other ways: during the Cultural Revolution, mediocrities tended to rise to the top. Now that they were faced with performing in front of foreign guests, the troupe managers took the route of expediency, and invited back anyone would could still perform, regardless of their political status. In the end, those who were chosen to perform were mostly those, like me, who had kept practicing discreetly while segregated or out on farms.

After such a long break, it was wonderful to be back on familiar ground. Perhaps this was a sign that life would move back into balance. The welcoming gala at the Friendship Cinema was a great success. All members of the troupe, including me, performed well. Two songs written by Sihanouk himself, "Lovely China" and "Oh Phnom Penh," pushed the show to its climax. Sihanouk stood up with a big smile, clapped with the rhythm and waved to the performers and audience.

At the end, Sihanouk went up to the stage and shook hands with each performer. His wife, the beautiful Madame Norodom Monineath Sihanouk, was at his side. Their kindness changed my attitude toward royals. Marshal Ye Jianying was the Chinese official from the Central Committee in attendance, accompanied by the activist Wang Hongwen, making his debut at a major event in Shanghai. In time, Wang would rise to infamy as one of the Gang of Four, a radical faction within the party led by Jiang Qing.

Shanghai, 1971: Resuming practice for a diplomatic event.

After the show, acrobatic diplomacy was again on the agenda. This helped improve the troupe's status. Sihanouk had not yet liberated his country, but he had liberated us. While most cultural organizations were still involved in hard labor in the rural areas, our troupe was in Shanghai preparing to perform for foreign guests. We had our practice time restored, and received an extra 10-yuan food allowance. At this time, the people in the two propaganda teams started to address us as "revolutionary artistic workers." However, I was in a special category. I continued to receive political denunciation, yet I was allowed to perform on the stage. The only reason they let me perform was that I was good at my work; otherwise, they would have kicked me to Timbuktu.

At the end of September 1971, cars of various makes appeared outside the Friendship Cinema over several days. Experience told me there must be a conference for the big shots. But why hadn't there been any signs of the city preparing for the National Day celebration on October 1? I waited with bated breath.

On October 6, Premier Zhou welcomed the Ethiopian emperor, Haile Selassie I, who was visiting Shanghai, where I met him for the second time. Even though we had staged another great performance, there was a stern atmosphere that could not be dispelled. Premier Zhou's face was serious, even as he accompanied the emperor in shaking hands with the performers. I started to worry, as the premier shook hands with me, about what was happening and why he wasn't his usual self. We were not to know that, at that time, Mao Zedong and Lin Biao were locked in a life-or-death struggle.

On September 13, a Trident airliner with Lin Biao and some others on board crashed in Öndörkhaan in Mongolia. There was no news coverage, not even a few words. However, there had been rumors: when Mao Zedong, in the company of only one interpreter, received Emperor Haile Selassie I, he was said to have told the old emperor that his close comrade-in-arms wanted to assassinate him. The emperor was reputed to have said in an off-hand manner, "Lin was only your comrade-in-arms—my own son plotted to overthrow me."

When the Lin Biao incident could not be covered up any longer, the central government issued a notice. Artists were gathered at the People's Theatre to hear a notice being read out by the propaganda teams. They had no explanation for why Lin Biao, the closest friend and supposed successor to Mao, would try to seize power from, sabotage and even assassinate Mao. Two years before, these same teams had proudly announced that Lin Biao had been named Mao's successor in the party's constitution, an innovative move in the international Communist movement. Why would Deputy Chairman Lin, who had been loyal from 1928 to September 1971, try to assassinate Chairman Mao?

The official line from the soldiers' propaganda team was that Lin Biao's anti-revolutionary process had been developing for a long time, and, thus, it had taken a long time to see through him. I sensed that the Cultural Revolution was indeed a live-or-die fight for power, using shiny words as a cover.

Lin's death signalled the beginning of the end of the Cultural Revolution. When I saw Mao's photo in the newspaper, I was shocked to see an old man. In 1972, another movement started, criticising Lin and Confucius, with the focus on an article Lin had written, the "571 Project Outline." In it, he stated that Mao's policy for making the country richer had made the people poorer. This helped answer one question: why China, a socialist country, was so poor. The outline said Mao was the modern version of the tyrant Emperor Qin Shi Huang. I was shocked by Lin's attack, as Mao was the Red Sun to all of us.

After reading the article, I felt justified in privately questioning a lot of things, including the great, glorious party and its leader.

Mao's actions became increasingly capricious. In 1972, China and the United States, out of their own strategic needs, established a formal diplomatic relationship. Richard Nixon's visit to China changed the world's political framework, outflanking the Soviet Union.

Amid these confusing signs, we in the troupe had to get to work. Premier Zhou issued an instruction to prepare an acrobatic show for the Nixons' visit to Shanghai—and no mistakes! Our troupe started preparing two months before the event, which was scheduled for the night of February 26, 1972. For security reasons, all performers were brought to the Pudong Hotel in Central Yan'an Road, which was affiliated with the Shanghai garrison. No outside contact would be allowed, nor any outings permitted. We could have a lunch break only in our rooms. On the day of the performance, we were taken to the venue at five in the afternoon. All was double-checked: the props, costumes, lighting and the curtains. There was heavy security in place along the route to the Friendship Cinema: all side roads were closed, and no windows in the houses along the way were to be opened.

After arriving backstage, I noticed that the guards were casually dressed, but looked very uncomfortable, their eyes constantly scanning. They did not know where to put their hands—sometimes they clenched their fists, sometimes they released and stretched their palms. I could tell these uneasy men were not normal guards but soldiers from the Ministry of Public Security, deployed at short notice.

We performed well and when we stood onstage at the end and saw Premier Zhou, Mr. and Mrs. Nixon and Henry Kissinger clapping heartily with smiles on their faces, we realized our efforts had not been in vain. The successful one-hour show somehow created a lighter environment for the upcoming signing of the Sino-US Shanghai Communiqué.

Our troupe returned to its role as an arm of Chinese diplomacy. We performed for Empress Farah Pahlavi of Iran, to whose visit the

Shanghai, 1972: Premier Zhou (center) applauding our acrobatic show at the Friendship Cinema with US president Richard Nixon (right) and his wife, Patricia (left).

Chinese government attached great importance. Fortunately, that one went smoothly—but others did not.

Our show to welcome a Chilean naval fleet was delayed when Wang Hongwen, the host of the pre-show banquet, requested that the Chilean party announce their anti-Soviet attitude. The chief commander of the Chilean fleet did not want to make any such announcement, and the atmosphere frosted over. Because of the delay caused by this stand-off, the performance started late. Luckily, the audience had been arranged, and they knew their political role in attending, so they waited as patiently as we did.

Another hiccup occurred when our troupe, along with the Shanghai Symphony Orchestra, staged a special program for a Romanian government delegation. The first half was the acrobatics and the second half was the revolutionary symphony *Shajiabang*. At the end of the show, Wang Hongwen stood up in the aisle and waited

Shanghai, 1972: In the second row, Empress Farah Pahlavi of Iran is in the center, behind the bouquet, while eighth from the left is Li Xiannian and eighth from the right is Zhang Chunqiao. I am twelfth from the left.

Shanghai, 1974: At a welcoming gala for to the Philippines First Lady Imelda Marcos.

for the Romanian representative to go onstage. The performers and the audience had been clapping for a while, and the Romanian guest still didn't stand up—he had fallen asleep. It was only after some prodding that he woke up and went onstage to shake the performers' hands. I didn't know whether his itinerary was too busy or the symphony was too gentle. We were never again on the same program with *Shajiabang*.

Mess-ups of various kinds were quite regular on these occasions, but none was more memorable than Japanese Prime Minister Tanaka Kakuei's visit to China. The United States had planned Nixon's visit to China without notifying their ally Japan, which upset Japanese politicians. To reverse a losing trend in foreign diplomacy, and to break through the conservative forces in Japan, Tanaka came to China in June 1972, signed a treaty and started a formal diplomatic relationship. Tanaka usually went to sleep early, so our show was one hour earlier than usual. At the scheduled time, Tanaka didn't appear. Just as the show was about to start, a TV journalist rushed into the hall and told everyone backstage that Tanaka had had too much to drink and was not coming.

We learned later that Premier Zhou had told Tanaka repeatedly, "Promises must be honored, and actions must lead to results."

Tanaka became excited over the success of his trip, but the Chinese mao-tai liquor was much stronger than his customary sake, and he couldn't handle it. At the end of the banquet, Zhang Chunqiao, one of Madame Mao's cronies, had said that as each must be responsible for sweeping the snow outside their house, everyone had to drain their cup. Tanaka had drained his.

At the theater, the stage supervisor announced, "The show is canceled for certain reasons. Remove your makeup, dismantle the stage, pack up."

15

ACROBATIC DIPLOMACY

The visits by the American and Japanese leaders to China in 1972 ended the "closed-door" policy of the Cultural Revolution. To further serve China's diplomatic needs, the central government decided to send acrobatic troupes overseas once more. The Shenyang troupe went to the United States, the national troupe went to the Middle East, and the Shanghai troupe went to Europe.

Before our trip to Europe, we tried to improve the troupe's weakest point—the stage design. We borrowed professional staff from the Shanghai People's Arts Theatre, the opera house, the Yue opera house, and the dancing school, and tried to utilize their expertise in creating a stage design with Shanghai characteristics. We invited Cheng Shifa, a famous painter, to design a poster for our performances in Europe. His *Spinning Plates* depicted a southern Chinese girl, in her ethnic costume, among lotus leaves blowing gently in the breeze, spinning eight plates. The poster had real Chinese charm.

However, the residue of the Cultural Revolution still hung over our efforts. Cheng had not yet been cleared on "political grounds," so the poster was not shown to the public. An expedient solution was found. Du Shixiang, an artist who had made a great contribution to stage design in the acrobatic field, was asked to use thin, transparent paper to trace Cheng's work. He painted a duplicate of *Spinning Plates,* bypassing the sensitive political issue. A beautiful poster by an anonymous artist was to enrich the tour of Europe.

Not long after the Chinese New Year in 1973, our troupe went to Beijing for pre-departure procedures. As in the past, we had to attend talks by relevant people from the central government about the countries we were to visit, and the Chinese government's foreign policy stance. This time, it was Yu Zhan, the deputy foreign minister who had just resumed office after being pulled down by the radicals, who spoke to us about foreign policy.

Yu was extremely careful with his words. For instance: we were visiting developed capitalist countries in Western Europe. Chairman Mao had said that they "resemble a dying person who is sinking fast, like the sun setting beyond the western hill." If Yu were to read this out, Mao's words would easily be disproved when we went there and were able to see with our own eyes. But if Yu omitted Mao's words, he would be in a very difficult situation. So he spoke in a broad sense: "The capitalist society has existed for a couple of hundred years now. It has a much longer history than our socialist society. If they appear to be stronger than us, that would hardly be surprising. However, we must see through the surface and recognize their dying reality. I believe that you, comrades, who have undergone the training and tests of the Cultural Revolution, have the ability to distinguish the difference between the two social systems."

In the past, I liked learning about the countries we were to visit. I had been an excited child. But this time, I did not get much out of the pre-departure talks. After all I had been through, I was now a hardened, cautious ex-prisoner. Whatever I thought, I could not open my mouth. I still believed in the project of restoring China's cultural self-esteem after the damage wrought by colonialism. But I also knew that the troupe management was only taking me on tour because I was too skillful to leave at home. If the propaganda teams had their wish, I would still be locked up.

Yu then changed the topic. "When abroad, make sure you respect the traditions and customs of the host country. It is not only a matter of courtesy, it is also of great importance in fulfilling the diplomatic task given to you. Don't make unnecessary demands on the hosts, especially regarding food. Eat whatever is provided. Don't be picky. I understand some female performers may not like lamb (an uncommon meat then in China), but what if the lamb comes in a dish? In order to have enough strength for your performance, you must eat it."

After all his careful career-preserving political correctness, and tiptoeing around various dangers, Yu concluded his talk with a bizarre instruction: "I am now making an announcement, and it is a rule. While having meals, eat with your mouth. Do not sniff your food before you eat it."

✦ ✳ ✱

The pre-departure performance was to be held at the Great Hall of the People. While we were busy loading our gear, a security officer, Liao, who had recently been appointed by the Ministry of Public Security, pointed at us and said, "How come your coats are just like the ones worn by the people receiving labor rehabilitation? Don't move around in these coats, people will think you are refugees!"

Looking at our coats, borrowed in Shanghai, with "Safety

Production" written on them, we were at a loss. One minute we had been receiving labor rehabilitation, the next we were being cautioned against looking like it. Appearances meant everything.

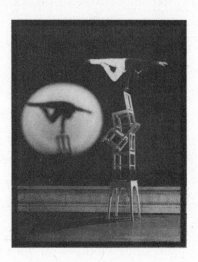

Shanghai, 1973: Performing a balancing act on our pre-departure performance on Chinese New Year.

On the day of the farewell show, we were invited to dinner at the Great Hall of the People. Watching us eat would be some of the most powerful officials in the country, and they might criticize us. There were about fifty of us, and we only occupied a small corner in the 10,000-person dining hall. The chopsticks on the tables were quite long. We were told that ivory chopsticks had been used, but were discontinued after foreign guests kept taking them home after their meals. The long chopsticks from Chairman Mao's home province of Hu'nan then became the usual utensils.

The Xiang-style food from Hunan Province, prepared by the top chefs in the country, was delicious, especially the spicy chicken and salted pork. However, pre-show nerves caused some of the troupe to lose their appetite, finish the meal in a rush and hurry off to prepare. Backstage, without the usual banter, was rather quiet. Performers were applying their makeup or helping with the props. Others were checking lights, backdrops and costumes. All realized the importance of this show.

Two of the future Gang of Four—Jiang Qing and Wang Hongwen—and the head of the army who would overthrow them, Marshal Ye Jianying, attended. Once they were seated, the show began. The frequent applause suggested it was a success. There were errors, as in any show. Pan, the bike-rider, as he had often done, fainted in the middle of the stage due to nerves. In the VIP seats, the secretary of our troupe heard Wang Hongwen say bluntly, "Pan was not bad in Shanghai. What was wrong with him tonight?"

"Why don't you go on the stage and have a go?" Marshal Ye responded.

As soon as we'd finished, the producer announced: "Stop what you are doing. Assemble in the foyer in the order of troupe leaders, performers, band, stage design and backstage workers. The leaders from the central government will be receiving us."

A journalist from the Xinhua News Agency's Shanghai branch made an announcement to those who wanted their photo taken with the leaders: "In order to protect Comrade Jiang Qing's eyes, it has been decided that no flash is allowed. It is quite dim in the foyer and it will not be fit for photo sessions. We hope you will understand." An actress before she married Mao Zedong, Comrade Jiang Qing was more conscious than most of how she looked in photographs.

Not long after we'd assembled, Jiang Qing, Ye Jianying and Wang Hongwen, with an entourage of secretaries in military green with badges, arrived in the foyer. They stopped 15 feet from us. A slim, well-cared-for Jiang Qing was in the prominent spot, with her head held high and her eyes glaring coldly. She was followed by a smiling Ye Jianying and Wang Hongwen.

We formed a queue and went up to shake hands with them. Jiang's hand held mine lightly and let go, a condescending frown on her face. Ye's hand was like that of a caring old man. When I shook hands with him, I was wondering which of his fingers had been broken when he banged the table while arguing about the Cultural Revolution with leftists. Wang Hongwen shook my hand with great strength. He knew how hard I had performed.

Beijing, 1973: This was taken just before my departure.
Glorifying my country was always on my mind.

• • •

In the early morning of March 25, 1973, the China Airlines airplane chartered for us with Jiang Qing's special permission departed from Beijing for Albania. We had a stopover at Kandahar, Afghanistan, to refuel. Our plane was the only one on the ground. Apart from us, there were no other passengers in the dilapidated departure hall, which was full of flies. One hour later, we continued our flight to Tirana, capital of Albania.

If I have a friend who knows me, even if he's thousands of miles
away, it's like he's with me.
Albania and China are thousands of miles apart
But our hearts are together.
Our friendship, formed during the revolutionary times, has
survived storms and the test of time.

This familiar Communist song, "We Are Real Friends," lingered in
my ears. Officials representing the local foreign affairs department,
education department, cultural department and friendship association were there to greet us, along with Liu Zhenhua, China's
ambassador to Albania, and a member of the Central Committee.
Standing on the steps leading down from the plane, seeing the singing and dancing on the ground, I was moved to see such a grand
welcoming gala for us. In China, only party or political delegations
from friendly countries received such attention.

Tirana was still cold in early spring, and not noisy as there were
few cars in the street. Thanks to this, I could breathe the fresh air
right down into my body. In front of the hotel stood a beautiful
grove of upright pines. Under the blue sky was a distant snow-
capped mountain. Seeing another country, after years of not
knowing if I would ever perform again, was like being born again.
What a glorious place! In the next three weeks, we traveled from
Tirana to five other cities, giving fifteen performances, and were
warmly welcomed by audiences and parades in each city.

Albania accorded our visit great political importance. On April
14, the full delegation, alongside the Chinese men's and women's
basketball teams, was received by Enver Hoxha, the first secretary of
the Albanian Labor party, at the Palace of Brigades. The captain of
the men's team, Qian Chenghai, sat next to me on the bus to the palace. We had met in Indonesia in 1963. He complained, "We've been

here three times, and have never been received by Hoxha. This is your first visit and you get to be received. I don't know whether we'd be here if it were not for you."

"You've been the captain for years now," I said. "To be received or not depends on the government's political needs. You should know that. It has nothing to do with which delegation you are with."

"Well, you have a point."

Tirana was not big, and we arrived at the Palace of Brigades in no time. Before we could have a closer look at the architecture, we were ushered into the reception hall by Liu, our security officer. We sat along two long tables to sample the delicious food. I listened to the conversation between two officials who spoke through an interpreter. They must have known each other quite well because they didn't beat about the bush. I heard the Albanian official say that clauses about religious freedom had been removed from their constitution. In China, Buddhist temples had been smashed, churches had been locked up, monks had been expelled and sacred scriptures had been burned. The smashing of the Four Olds included being anti-religion. But the Chinese constitution always contained the clause that religions could be practiced freely. The Albanian revolution, it seemed, was at least more honest than the Chinese one.

Hoxha arrived, a tall, fair man with a rosy complexion. He was handsome with a high nose and big eyes, and he looked energetic. After being seated, he asked how the Chinese comrades were feeling about Albania, and praised the contribution the Shanghai Acrobatic Troupe had made to the friendship between the two countries. The reception was not long, most of it being taken up with arranging the positions for a group photo with Hoxha and more than a hundred people.

That evening, a welcome dinner was arranged at our hotel. We arrived before the hosts. Seeing raw lamb brains in the entrée, Ma,

Tirana, 1973: One of the group photos taken at the reception dinner. Enver Hoxha is at the center of the second row from the front. I am in the sixth row from the front, fourth on the right.

the interpreter with the Chinese embassy, said, "There will be a politburo member attending tonight." Soon after, Abdyl Këllezi, Albanian Labor Party Politburo member, chairman of the State Planning Commission and also chairman of the Sino-Albanian Friendship Association, arrived. The atmosphere was excellent that night; we ended up holding hands and dancing around the long dining table.

China's influence, through manufactured imports, was everywhere. I saw many Forever and Phoenix bicycles, brands made in Shanghai. In China, we needed a voucher to buy a bicycle. I had sent in my application months before, and heard nothing. The Sun-Oriented thermos in our hotel was also the most popular Chinese brand during the Cultural Revolution. We visited the Berat District to see the Mao Zedong United Textile Factory, which had been established with Chinese assistance. We learned that China provided not only the equipment but also technicians from Shanghai.

Fier was the second city we visited. At the welcome dinner, an Albanian officer from the education and arts department asked Yuan Donglin, the director of our delegation, whether it was possible for Comrade Xue Jingjing to stay and work as an acrobatic expert in Albania. Such a matter could not be decided on the spot, and would require complex levels of approval. Yuan passed the ball to me: "We need to see what Xue Jingjing thinks of this."

I had heard their conversation from the next table. I also knew they were providing me with a headache. I couldn't say yes, but nor could I say no too bluntly. So, in a roundabout way, I said, "It is a great honor that I am being invited to stay and work as an expert. To contribute to the friendship between China and Albania is something I must do. However, as we have just started our tours in Europe, would it be possible to wait until our programs are finished, and we can decide after seeking approval from the relevant authorities?"

The next morning, when I arrived at the theater to practice, an Albanian interpreter who had studied at the Beijing Foreign Languages Institute said to me, grim-faced, "Comrade Xue Jingjing, you haven't studied thoroughly Chairman Mao's article 'In Memory of Norman Bethune.' You lack the spirit of internationalism."

My insides shrivelled. My experiences during the Cultural Revolution had left me with a deep fear of the thing called politics, where every step could be a fatal mistake.

On April 16, we boarded a Romanian Air Transport Ilyushin Il-18. Just as we had thirteen years before, we needed to chew fruit candies handed out by the air hostess to reduce the pain in our ears caused by the cabin pressure. I don't know whether that plane was overdue for service or it should have been retired, but we had a bumpy ride in the perfect bright sky. As unpleasant as the flight was, at least it was short, and we landed safely at Bucharest airport.

At the airport, we saw the frequent landing and taking off of civilian airplanes, and long queues of passengers through customs. An "opening-up" policy had been adopted, especially toward the West, to attract investment for the five-star hotels under construction, and for the private hire cars parked along the streets. Bucharest was a booming city. I could tell that Romania was trying hard to rid itself of the poverty associated with socialism. Romania had been

Sinaia, 1973: At Peleş Castle, also known as the Summer Palace because the royal family lived there in summer, on a daytrip from Bucharest.

navigating carefully at the border of Soviet control, managing to open up to the West while avoiding the tragedy that had befallen Hungary and Czechoslovakia.

We performed at Circus Globus, situated in a lush green belt. The Romanian audiences were very interested, and we had to add a seventeenth show to our schedule. Apart from the few performances that fell during Easter, all tickets were sold out in no time. On Good Friday, with the audience halved, we young Chinese, who had no idea about Easter, became confused. How could religion prevail in such a way in a country that believes in Marxism-Leninism? A consular officer who had been accompanying us explained, "Many Romanians practice religion, including some high officials in the party. From Easter Friday to Sunday, they are very busy with religious activities. On the way to the hotel tonight, you will see people holding candles in the streets, which is part of their religious tradition. Don't be sad about the low attendance over these few days. After Easter, all will go back to normal."

We did see a lot of people holding candles on the way to the hotel later that evening. In China, the party had called on its members to "make revolution in the depths of the soul," an attempt to clear any religious sensibility out of the Chinese people. But socialism did not have to be the same for every population.

On May 8, we arrived in Paris. It was spring, with beautiful flowers, huge trees with canopies, and the Seine running tranquilly through the city. People from all around the world were on the streets, and I could feel their ease in this highly advanced capitalist country. Jean Charbonnel, the minister of industrial and scientific development, and his wife attended the premiere performance on May 10 at a Paris sports stadium, along with an audience of 3000. A week later, Valéry Giscard d'Estaing, minister for the economy and a future president of France, came to watch the show. There were so many spectators that the stadium car park filled up and many had to take the Metro.

I had looked forward to seeing traces of the history of France, those historic places where figures such as Napoleon Bonaparte had been, the museums, the Place de la Concorde and its obelisk. Our leaders made sure we saw appropriate socialist monuments in this capitalist city: we visited the Communards' Wall and the memorial to the anti-fascist war. A plaque at the Communards' Wall had inscriptions dedicated to those who died in the class struggle between the twenty-first and twenty-eighth of May 1871. At the Père-Lachaise Cemetery, we saw the tomb of Eugène Pottier, who composed the "Internationale." In front of the 15-foot high, 20-foot wide Communards' Wall, that great song played in my ears.

Paris, 1973: Beside the tomb of French revolutionary Eugène Pottier at Père-Lachaise Cemetery.

Visiting these places, I felt the strength of France's tolerant nature. It was this tolerance that enabled the preservation of ideologically diverse sites. History was preserved regardless of the temporary political winds. A nation, or a people, without a complete history could not be considered great.

The night after the visit to the Communards' Wall, I had a strange dream. Li Yuhe, the hero in *The Red Lantern* (a Beijing opera), and Hong Changqing, the party representative in *The Red Detachment of Women* (a ballet), sang the "Internationale" as they slowly walked to their execution ground. I heard Pottier say to Karl Marx, "In China, the 'Internationale' is only being considered as a departure song for those who are to be executed. They have long lost faith in the reality of the 'Internationale.'"

When I woke up, I was disturbed by my dream. Was it really true that one suppresses a thought in the daytime, and turns it into a dream at night?

During our visit, the French Communist Party requested that we pass a message to the central government. Yuan Donglin responded: "We are only an artistic troupe. For matters concerning the relationship between the parties, please contact the International Liaison Department of the CPC Central Committee." Everywhere we went, we could not put a toe out of line.

It was a pity that we could not visit the island of If, near Marseille, known to us from the book *The Count of Monte Cristo*. There had been a plan to visit, but we were only allowed to see the island from a mile away because, Yuan Donglin said, "I am sure there will be foreign women enjoying the sun in only their bikinis, which will have a bourgeois influence on our troupe."

At the end of May, when we went to Rome, Shen Ping, China's ambassador to Italy, told us, "You may go around the Vatican in a bus, but you must not get out of the bus. Furthermore, you must not go into the Vatican, because you may cause unnecessary diplomatic trouble." So we circled the Vatican in a tour bus and stopped along the white line that was the border of the tiny country. I saw St. Peter's Basilica and the Square, which brought back distant memories of the religious practice allowed during my infancy at Xin Puyu Tang Orphanage. But these great ecclesiastical sights were only permissible through the bus window.

We were moving from country to country so quickly we soon grew tired. The plan was for a five-day break in Paris, but it was shortened to three, during which we underwent political studies, full of criticism and self-criticism. No rest. All the usual nit-picking

*Milan, 1973: Outside the iconic Milan
cathedral, Duomo di Milano.*

small issues were stirred up, even personal attacks and grudges from the Cultural Revolution, which made me sick.

Already tired due to the constant changes of location, a bout of diarrhea rendered me seriously exhausted. But I had no choice but to hold on and finish the tour. We had a warm reception in the spectacular principality of San Marino, even amid heavy rain; unfortunately, my condition didn't improve until we were on the plane from there to Malta. When we were descending, I saw the island was the shape of a fish. Malta is a serene, beautiful place, with sunshine on its beaches, waves lapping on the shores, and colorful flowers surrounding big palm trees. Ours was the first visit by Chinese artists to Malta. Our tour guide, a historian, told us about a temple in which male voices carried farther than female voices. We could not believe that until we went there and gave it a test. "Oh, it's a very strange temple," some people said. "We've never seen anything like it."

. . .

On July 3, people from all over the British Isles crowded into London's Coliseum Theatre, hung with the Chinese national flag, to see our performance. Among the audience were Prince Richard, Duke of Gloucester, Prime Minister Edward Heath, shadow minister Denis Healey, the future prime minister James Callaghan, Reg Birch from the Communist Party of Britain (Marxist-Leninist), and Song Zhiguang, China's ambassador to the United Kingdom. A meeting had been held before the show to stress its importance with so many VIPs in attendance. After the show, Prince Richard and Edward Heath attended a reception for us. The prime minister had a friendly chat with us, and later wrote to Song Zhiguang, "It was a great pleasure to watch the performance. I hope the applause and the excellent commentaries in the newspapers have assured you of this. It was very obvious that the whole audience sang the praises of the show, and we are very happy to have the Chinese acrobats performing in the UK."

The success of the show and the content of this letter demonstrated that the unpleasant past, especially the burning of a British liaison office by some rogue Red Guards in China, was a page that had been turned. Our eleven shows in London sold out very quickly. When an extra show was announced, a long line formed outside the box office.

We visited Highgate Cemetery in the northwest of London to again pay our respects to Karl Marx in his resting place. We also went back to Marx's seat in the British Museum, and to Westminster. As I stood in front of the symbol of Western parliamentary democracy, I was full of thoughts about the political system in China. In western countries, the two parties follow the same general capitalist line. In China, there is only one party, but it goes on two lines, and

London, 1973: At the tomb of Karl Marx in Highgate Cemetery.
The most important thing is to know how to transform the world.

Germany, 1973: The inscription on Engels's commemoration
tablet says, "Here was once the birth place of F. Engels, the great
son of Wuppertal, one of the founders of scientific socialism."

between these lines there is a life-or-death struggle. I had witnessed the severe in-party fighting and seen Chairman Mao's two designated successors, Liu Shaoqi and Lin Biao, purged.

After the UK, we traveled to West Germany. The German audiences were different from those in other countries. They not only clapped their hands, but shouted and stomped their feet. I was a little disturbed by the passionate, high-decibel response while I was performing a handstand. I was reassured later that the cacophony meant my performance was excellent.

While in Cologne, we took a side trip to Wuppertal to visit the house of Friedrich Engels, a two-story building refurbished in 1970 for Engels's 150th birthday. Nine hundred feet away was the site of the house in which Engels had been born in 1820; the house itself had been destroyed by Allied bombs. A tablet had been erected there with an inscription. This tablet, the memorial museum, and the streets and parks which had been named after Engels demonstrated capitalist Germany's tolerance for socialist views. You didn't see any acknowledgment of capitalist heroes in China!

On the bank of the Rhine river, a three-story orange building was commemorated as Ludwig van Beethoven's residence. The head of his statue in the hall on the ground floor was raised slightly as if contemplating something, and his deep eyes seemed to follow me throughout my visit. Behind a glass window were some yellow manuscripts and a pair of simple copper hearing aids, which told the story of how Beethoven suffered after he lost his hearing, and how he fought hard against the cruelty of life to create so many masterpieces. Standing on the first floor, I was shocked to see that each of the ivory keys on the piano had been dented by use. I stood there in silence, not knowing how to express my feelings.

After three performances in West Germany's biggest port city, Hamburg, we flew to West Berlin, the focus of the European

Cold War. Our security was a major concern and the West Berlin government dispatched four big guards to accompany our troupe at all times. One of them attached himself closely to Liu, who was in charge of security, but whose camouflage identity was "secretary to the Youth League." The big guard's presence certainly gave Liu's game away.

Security at night was especially crucial. We stayed on the fourth and the fifth floors of our hotel. We would go up in the lift in batches, and were not allowed to use the lift to go up or down again during the night. We were only allowed to go between the fourth and the fifth floors using the stairs, in case any people from East Germany or the Soviet Union got to us in the lift. Security guards with handguns provided overnight protection. In 1956, seventeen years before, when the Shanghai Acrobatic Troupe performed in East Berlin, the performers had been told to be cautious of harm that might be caused by the Western powers. Now, it was the opposite: we needed to be vigilant for harm that might come from the Eastern powers.

The 96-mile-long path of the Berlin Wall was a must-see. On the bus, I kept my eyes wide open in case I missed it. This wall had been the focus of the struggle between East and West, and so many incidents had happened there. The bus driver slowed, to show us the graffiti on the wall. I wondered how long this wall could hold up against the Western imperialists. John F. Kennedy had called it "the most obvious and vivid demonstration of the failures of the Communist system." Was the Berlin Wall really that important that it determined the life and death of Communism? I had no answer.

The dream of Konrad Adenauer, the then West German chancellor, was to restore Berlin as the capital of Germany. That was a dream shared by the people of West Berlin. When we visited the subways, a university student who acted as our tour guide told us,

"The West Berlin subways are all in place, and the connection points with the East Berlin subways have also been designed. We are now working on the preliminaries for the connection of the two subway systems."

The connection had only another sixteen years to wait!

* * *

It was late August when we arrived in Istanbul, a city sitting on two continents, controlling the Bosphorus strait. On our third day in Turkey, the local newspaper published news about the Tenth National Congress of the Chinese Communist Party, with a photo of Wang Hongwen and Zhou Enlai flanking Mao Zedong. We were curious about this photo and tried to guess what message was being sent out. I had my own interpretation. Before we departed, Wang Hongwen had come to our practice venue to see us, and said something cryptic: "Due to my current position, it would not be convenient for me to see you off at the airport. I'll bid you farewell here."

Seeing this photo, I understood what Wang had meant. His rapid ascent was astonishing, and would only continue. Later, during our first performance for foreign heads of state on our return, Wang Xiuzhen from the Shanghai Revolutionary Committee came backstage during the interlude. She told us: "In 1972, when Comrade Wang Hongwen was promoted to Beijing to work, we all believed he would get rapid promotion, but none of us imagined that he would be promoted to deputy chairman of the party, so high and so quickly."

From March to August 1973, we visited nine countries, giving dozens and dozens of performances. Driven to overcome fatigue by my duty to keep glorifying my country, I held on for another four weeks in Istanbul and Ankara. Fahri Korutürk, the Turkish president, and his wife came to see the premiere, while Prime Minister Naim Talu came to our show in Ankara. Again we performed extra shows to meet popular demand. The applause, the gasps and the flowers from the audience made us proud. I was a performer, and even though my body was spent, my heart was happy.

*Ankara, 1973: I was exhausted by this point, but
buoyed by the response to our performances.*

On September 26, totally exhausted after six months of uninterrupted touring and performing, we dragged ourselves onto a chartered flight from Ankara via Ürümqi to Shanghai. What a pleasure it was to see the blue sky from the plane window and to think that I was going home. However, when I remembered the Shanghai where the Cultural Revolution was still going on, where everyone was "glad to fight others with delight," my mood started to wither.

After returning home and going into preparations for our next tour, we received a very welcome international guest. Edward

Heath, who had recently resigned as Britain's prime minister, met with Chairman Mao and Deputy Premier Deng Xiaoping in Beijing, and his words of praise for our troupe appeared in the newspaper: "Like many of my compatriots, I very much enjoyed the successful shows performed by the Shanghai Acrobatic Troupe."

When he came to Shanghai, I was invited to the welcome dinner hosted by the Shanghai Revolutionary Committee. I had been invited to such dinners from time to time to satisfy diplomatic needs, but never such a high-level one; I was very nervous as I got dressed. My clothing could be divided into three categories: the blue-grayish daily dress that we commoners wore, worn-out clothing for rural labor, and formal dress for diplomatic events. The government paid for the formal outfits, and mine was a tailor-made navy-gray wool Zhongshan-style tunic suit. Two or three hours before the dinner, the Shanghai militia had closed off the streets surrounding the Shanghai Exhibition Center. As I rode my bike toward the roadblocks, I saw militia wearing brand-new blue workers' uniforms printed with "Safety Production"—the same hard-labor uniform I had worn not so long ago.

In China, a government official, no matter how low his level, had an air about him. I got off my bike in front of such an official and showed him my invitation. He took a dubious look at me, and then back at the invitation, before gesturing to his men to allow a small path for me to pass through. As soon as I had pushed my bike through, I heard a militia man saying, "Why was he let through? Didn't those above say not to let anyone through?"

Having passed that blockade, I got back on my bike. The usually busy Nanjing Road had become quiet. What a strange feeling, after being on the outside all my life, to be inside the cordon of power.

The dinner, hosted by Ma Tianshui of the revolutionary committee, was at the dining hall above the Friendship Cinema. Ma was rather chubby and his Zhongshan suit didn't fit him well; he looked funny accompanying Edward Heath into the banquet hall.

The atmosphere at the dinner was friendly. After Sir Edward—as he would later become—gave a speech, I was told to go up and propose a toast to him. When I approached him, he stood. After I was introduced as the "main performer in last year's tour to the UK," I raised my glass and said, "Drink to those good memories the Honorable Mr. Heath has from when we visited the UK last year. Drink to the more frequent exchanges of artists between our two countries. Drink to our friendship, and to the success of Mr. Heath's visit to China."

My cup, which contained mao-tai, clinked with Heath's, which contained wine.

16

JAPAN

To celebrate the one-year anniversary of the sister city relationship between Shanghai and Yokohama, the Sino-Japan Friendship Association asked for a performing troupe to visit seven Japanese cities, including Yokohama.

Apart from the usual preparatory sessions, this time we had extra sessions of "dialogue" at the behest of the Shanghai Revolutionary Committee. The so-called dialogue training was to teach us how to carry out conversations in Japan in case we should find ourselves speaking with friendly, or unfriendly, hosts who may have questions about what the past eight years had done to China's politics, economy, culture and arts, and morality. We were required to respond that China's situation was "grand" (not just good, but grand!). In a world with fast communications, this was making us objects of ridicule.

We started to practice the set text, like a bunch of parrots. Each week, we spent one or two afternoons on dialogues. Here are some examples:

Q: Why, during the Cultural Revolution, did they want to bring down Liu Shaoqi?

A: Liu Shaoqi betrayed the plans of the proletarian revolution, and had become the biggest capitalist roader in the party. That's why Chairman Mao mobilized the people of China and overthrew him.

Q: What's the purpose of the practice of criticizing Lin and Confucius?

A: Lin Biao, like Confucius, was trying to promote the return of feudalism. That's why we needed to criticize him.

Q: Is the Cultural Revolution promoting the development of productivity?

A: Of course it promotes the development of productivity, because we, the proletariat class, are the representatives of the advanced productivity.

Q: Was the "smashing of the Four Olds" at the beginning of the Cultural Revolution a movement that detached China from its history?

A: The "smashing of the Four Olds" is a revolution that demonstrates the separation of our proletariat from the mentality, behavior and moral standards of all the exploiting classes in history.

Q: Are you leading a happy life?

A: Of course we are happy. Compared with the working-class people in the old society, our life is like that in Heaven and theirs was like that in Hell. Not only do we feel content materially, we feel very happy spiritually. We have turned the situation around and have become the masters of our country.

Such Q&A sessions had been distilled into our brains to prevent loss of face. But we were not machines to record and replay messages. We did have thoughts. I hated this dialogue training, just like I hated the slogans on the walls, such as "We must believe in the masses. We must believe in the party. These are the two fundamental theories. If we doubt these two theories, nothing will be achieved." After my experiences during the Cultural Revolution, I could only shake my head—but of course I had to keep my thoughts to myself.

Luckily I didn't speak any Japanese, and could not have any conversations with Japanese-speaking people. Those we mingled with were friendly to China and never asked embarrassing questions. The dialogue training was not only dumb, but a waste of time.

In 1974, commercial flights between China and Japan had to go through Hong Kong. Our flight from Shanghai to Tokyo was an exception. It only took two hours, without any time difference, and I felt quite relaxed. As soon as we landed in Japan, we felt the bustling efficiency of the place. We were rushed to a big bus outside the Narita airport to go to our hotel in Yokohama, where we had a brief rest before setting up at the theater for several days of performances.

Our performances took place in premises controlled by Shimizu Masao, director of the Matsuyama Ballet. The first time I heard about this ballet company was in the 1960s, when the Shanghai Ballet copied the Matsuyama's *The White-Haired Girl,* adapted from a Chinese movie. During the Cultural Revolution, it became one of only eight model operas that were allowed to be performed in China. Shimizu was a decent man and he looked after everything in detail. His assistant, Oba, who was in charge of gear and equipment, did an amazing job, recording precisely where we put the big cases of our equipment in sequence for the show. When we arrived in Tokyo, Nagoya, Osaka, Kobe, Shimonoseki and Fukuoka, all our cases were arranged in their exact locations and order. Oba's, or should I say Japan's, work ethic and attitude must have been a key to the country's economic miracle.

Japan's transportation system was advanced, especially the shinkansen, the core railway line that linked the major cities. Sitting on the "bullet train," I relaxed and thought to myself, if the whole world could use the shinkansen, we would be less tired when arriving in new cities.

Our Japanese hosts had squeezed all sorts of activities into our schedule, which I enjoyed a lot. Japan is surrounded by sea and, with few natural resources, had focused on shipbuilding. It was because of this that Japan was able to start the Pacific War and challenge the United States for supremacy at sea. Before visiting a Japanese shipyard, I thought I had enough knowledge to imagine the size of Japan's shipbuilding industry. However, when I stood in front of an unfinished 260,000-ton crude-oil tanker, I was dumbfounded. That was totally beyond my imagination, and a living lesson in modern industry. Even though China won the war and Japan lost, it took only two decades for Japan to catch up with the world, and become a leading country in terms of economy, industry and education. Its economy had long overtaken China's. It took a tremendous effort for China to produce a ship of 10,000 tons, while Japan could build this 260,000-ton ship. We felt awed but also embarrassed.

Japan's agricultural sector was dominated by small-scale farming. I had thought small-scale agriculture, land reform and

Tokyo, 1974: Here I am performing with a ladder.

communal farming groups were developed in China, so I was very curious when we were shown a Japanese farm. Walking into a farmer's house, with a courtyard and tatami (bamboo mats) on the floor, we were surprised to find the house so spacious, accommodating the whole fifty-person delegation. This farmer belonged to one of three families that had formed a collective. He came out to welcome us, while the ladies ran back and forth serving tea. The host introduced members from the other two families, who bowed to us extravagantly. They told us, "After the land reform, we found it not proper to work individually. So we tried to help each other with funds and labor. We formed a communal support group and started to grow flowers."

These three families were operating a greenhouse, using electricity to provide light and heat to control the growth of the flowers. They maintained a fresh flower warehouse that provided flowers in both peak and low season. A strong Japanese economy had increased the demand for fresh flowers, which in turn increased the income for these three families. Expansion of their scale of production was on the agenda. Inhaling the fragrance of the flowers in their super-efficient greenhouse, seeing the confidence in the hosts' eyes, I could appreciate their passion and the success of their system.

At a post-show function in Osaka, a scholarly, bald monk wearing a Western-style suit came to make toasts to us. He introduced himself: "I am the abbot of the temple which you are going to visit tomorrow." He then turned and introduced his wife, who was behind him.

After this meat-eating, wife-taking monk went away, we immediately "attacked" our interpreter, who had received education in China and had returned to Japan in the early stages of the Cultural Revolution. We asked him, "How come in Japan your monks are so slack, and they are not being restricted by the old precepts?"

He replied: "Isn't China the same? In 1964 when I was attending university in Sichuan, I was assigned to participate in the Four Olds clearance movement in areas where there were Tibetan people. Those lamas who had been expelled from their temples had to work and provide for themselves. They had to participate in manual labor, and there was a demand for them to get married. I've seen lamas with several wives."

The conversation was veering onto hazardous ground. I chipped in: "There is no use commenting negatively on the Japanese monks or the Tibetan monks. Let's just go tomorrow and see how different the Japanese temple is from the Chinese ones."

China had made its own contributions to the greatness of Japan, but a long time ago. In Nara, we visited Toshodaiji Temple, which was built in the time of the Tang dynasty. The guide told us the temple was built in commemoration of the successful voyage to Japan by the Chinese monk Jianzhen, who had tried and failed five times before succeeding in getting there. He introduced Chinese culture and Buddhist precepts to Japan, and had overseen the building of famous temples in Nara and Kyoto. "Master Jianzhen contributed greatly in the introduction of the Chinese civilization to Japan," the guide concluded, making us feel a little less inferior.

Our political staff were eager to keep our minds from straying toward envy of capitalist Japan. One night, when we were returning from a performance, we saw a homeless man covered with cardboard. One of the political staff said, "Look, this is the ugly part of capitalism. From inside the doors of the rich come the aromas of meat and wine; however, outside the doors, there are people starving to death. This is a social phenomenon that is inevitable in capitalist societies. Not only did we see the colorful side of capitalism, we must also see these people who have been exploited by this system, living a miserable life."

Nagoya, 1974: In a hotel, contemplating the differences between Japan and China.

Osaka, 1974: Meeting a monk. The Buddha is an enlightened being. We can learn from all beings. I am on the far right in this picture.

This political staffer did nothing useful on the tour, but he never missed an opportunity to deride Japan. None of us paid him much attention.

The sight of cars parked in multi-story stations and of sports facilities on building roofs brought home to me how Japan's history had been defined by the lack of space. A country on a narrow strip of land, with limited resources, Japan invaded China to increase its space for survival. The war ended with the nuclear attacks on Hiroshima and Nagasaki, and in the end it was the Japanese people who suffered most. Definitely not the outcome the political leaders had foreseen. That knowledge wearied me further of China's ongoing political interference in our lives. During our time in Japan, we would temporarily forget the obligation to denigrate Liu Shaoqi and Lin Biao. Then we would be hit by our political officer with: "You must be actively involved in the criticism of Lin Biao and the Confucius movement, to transform your worldview." In the land where totalitarian ideology had failed so disastrously, all of that badgering indoctrination suddenly rang very hollow.

* * *

A return visit from Japanese artists gave me fresh insights into my own country. Japan's "NEW Production Seat" theater group, led by director Mayama Miho, was a left-leaning organization in sympathy with China's use of artistic groups to advance political aims. A year after our visit to Japan, they came to China to perform their revolutionary shows on the dilapidated stage of the Youth Palace.

I was part of their escort on a visit to Malu Commune, a showcase village on the northwest outskirts of Shanghai. This commune was nothing like the rural places I had worked in! Green fields with prospects of a good harvest, and buildings with bricks and tiles demonstrated good design. The presenter, a female commune member in her thirties, was impressive, even if her Shanghai dialect eluded the interpreter sent from Beijing, so that a relay had to be carried out to translate her words into official Mandarin and then into Japanese. The Japanese delegation members were amazed by this process.

When the Japanese performed, the members of the commune watched intently, clapping politely, with appreciative expressions, yet without screaming or loud talking. They must have done this often. After the show, accompanying the guests to see a farmer's home, I heard a journalist from the Xinhua News Agency mumbling to herself, "I've been to this house nine times. Why not visit a new place?"

So this had all been specially arranged. I should have known. At the next model community on the itinerary, Caoyang New Village, a fat middle-aged woman recited a well-rehearsed introduction, singing the praises of the Communist Party and the government. She introduced us to a family of four, with three generations: a grandmother, mother and father, and baby son. Their house was less than 65 square feet and very tidy. The old lady was looking after her lovely grandson, who was just about to talk. The young Japanese performers tried to hold him, and the atmosphere was warm and lively.

The vegetable stalls were the main show of the day, with red-armband-wearing retired workers keeping order. The smiling saleswomen in pure white uniforms were a contrast to the usual greasy uniforms and evil stepmother faces in real shops. I was thinking they might all be actors.

What was more amazing to me was the long-time-no-see fresh vegetables and live fish and shrimp. This was a modern Chinese version of a Potemkin village! Back in eighteenth-century Russia, Grigory Potemkin built some beautiful but fake castles on the sides of roads that Empress Catherine II would be traveling, to please her. What a shame we were showing this obvious fraud to the Japanese. Japan was a country with advanced information technology, so they would have known the basic situation in China. Showing them these model villages—a demonstration to save face—was only going to embarrass us.

That night, we went to the Youth Palace, whose previous name was Dashijie, or "a place famous for entertainment." At that time, with a 20-cent entrance fee, one could go in at noon and come out at ten pm, having seen each and every form of show in China. The saying was, "If you haven't been to the Dashijie, then you haven't been to Shanghai." During the Cultural Revolution, the performers had been forced out to the rural areas to "fix the earth" and have their minds transformed, and the Dashijie had been taken over by some performing teams chosen and assembled by the radicals.

The plan was to have a little discussion first, and then invite the Japanese guests to perform. Not long after the discussion had started, there was a blackout. Without any emergency backup lights, we had to wait in the dark. To break the awkwardness, one of the female radicals took the opportunity to start an onslaught of criticism: "Look, in the old society, the capitalists only wanted to make profits and they neglected the maintenance of the basic facilities. Tonight, we are the victims."

It had been twenty-five years since the capitalists had left the premises. I felt ashamed of the female radical's outburst, but I couldn't know how our Japanese guests felt because of the darkness. The lights came back on, and our discussion resumed. The focus of the Chinese host was the inferiority of the past society and the glory of the new China. Someone said, "In the old society, the performers here were exploited by the capitalists and hooligans. In the new society, these performers are able to be the new masters."

Someone else said, "Now the revolutionary arts workers are truly liberated. The Dashijie has now been renamed the Youth Palace, and it has become the most important battlefield of propaganda. We have our struggle sessions here against the capitalist roaders in the party."

After the Japanese delegation went home, I received a courtesy gift, a traditional handcrafted Japanese doll, from Mayama Miho. However, I was aware that even if it was a token, I could not reply in private. That was an ironclad regulation. I knew how much trouble "foreign connections" could get me into.

17

LIFE AFTER MAO

Deng Xiaoping had fallen in and out of favor with Chairman Mao over the years. When Deng was rehabilitated in April 1973, he started to implement measures to restore the national economy, rebuked the Cultural Revolution enthusiasts and paid more attention to the welfare of the people. As soon as Deng became popular, however, the Left began to criticize him again, a constant diatribe reported in newspapers, television and radio.

Like most Chinese who had experienced cruel attacks and struggles, who had seen many comrades purged, and who could see no end to this Cultural Revolution, I felt disgusted. The return of Deng Xiaoping had reignited the hopes of the common people, who were looking forward to normal, peaceful lives. With the increased shouting against Deng in official media, our hopes started to wane. Like many common people, I spent the year of 1975 in great uncertainty about the direction our nation was taking.

As always, I turned inwards, to my art. For several years, my goal had been unwavering: to master Ocinsky's handstand on a revolving platform. I renewed my commitment after coming back from Japan, but sensed that the attacks on Deng signaled a return of the extremes of the Cultural Revolution. I kept looking through the darkness in hope of seeing the stars. What I could do best was lose myself in practice, and forget the headache of class struggle. I focused on the state of high achievement, a pure land hidden in my heart. While practicing, my new motto of "Don't look up, don't look down, don't look back, and don't look around"—which I had adopted while in custody in 1970—shut out everything but my work.

In the troupe, we had some time for practice every day, but not enough for me. I was already twenty-eight and was about to reach, maybe pass, a performer's peak years. I did not want any regrets later in life. I had the physical abilities to surpass Ocinsky; I just needed time to practice, and a platform that could both revolve and be raised and lowered. This hydraulic device would cost more than was available, but without the rotating platform, I could not take the final step.

I approached Xu, the captain of the workers' propaganda team. Xu was a decent man and hadn't been brainwashed by the class struggles. He had been on our 1973 tour of Europe, he saw how hard we worked, and he was sympathetic toward us performers.

"I want to try to do the handstand on a revolving platform," I told him, explaining everything I had in mind about this.

"That's impossible. It is a foreign show. How could you do that?" It was an answer I had expected, given the anti-foreign atmosphere during the Cultural Revolution.

"Acrobatics is an international performing art," I replied. "The show belongs to the one who can perform best. Today, we may say that the show belongs to the Soviet Union. Tomorrow, people may say it belongs to China."

"Why?"

"Tomorrow, I will surpass Ocinsky," I said with great confidence.

"Why are you so sure?" Xu was not so sure!

"Ocinsky had reached the pinnacle of his career," I said. "Because of his age, he could not perform any other outstanding tricks, but I still have potential. He lost one arm in the war, and he definitely would have had all sorts of limitations in training. I have both my arms intact, and certainly I have more flexibility than he had in training. My handstand is better than his, and I don't have to re-invent the wheel he has already invented. I only need to think about ways to increase the level of skill, improve on what he has already achieved, combine the technical skills with the performing art, and make this part of China's handstand."

Xu was looking more interested. I went on to quote some of the popular sayings of the time.

"More importantly, I am a Chinese who is committed to assisting China's effort to stand in the forest of all nations in the world. Chairman Mao has said, 'The Chinese have the courage, the ability. We must catch up and surpass those world leaders.' Comrade Xu, now all I need is your support. Please allocate funding for me to produce the platform."

"How much?" Xu was beginning to bend.

"Around three thousand yuan."

"Oh, my goodness!" He threw his hands up. My heart sank. "That much? I could only approve dozens of yuan, or up to a couple of hundred." Then he relented a little. "Your application is huge, and I'll have to discuss it with the leaders and then make a decision."

Hearing this, I knew there was at least hope, so I added, with a big smile, "Rest assured, the money won't be spent in vain."

Not long after, Xu came to me and said, "Seeing that you've been practicing very hard, and you have a good command of what you do, we approve your application. Don't let us down. Also, you must have the correct political views while practicing. Not only should you practice well, you must involve yourself in the political movements, too."

From the end of 1974, I started to busy myself with the design of the platform. I studied theories of mechanics and hydraulics, and worked on many drawings. My days were very busy and I felt happier than I had in years. With the assistance of technicians and mechanics, the platform was finally built after months of strenuous effort. In late 1975, I started to practice on it. Even though I was exhausted every day, sweat pouring off me, it was the sweat of hard work and happiness. I felt my potential was belatedly being brought out.

*   *   *

I could never practice in a vacuum. In modern Chinese history, 1976 was a year that deserves a lot of ink.

On January 8, Premier Zhou Enlai died. The whole country fell into mourning. On April 4, which was the Pure Brightness Festival, a day for the Chinese to commemorate the deceased, people voluntarily gathered in Tiananmen Square to pay their final respects to Premier Zhou—and also to vent their anger at ten years of the Cultural Revolution by parading two slogans: "The people are not stupid" and "The people will not be bullied."

The next day, April 5, there was a crackdown on the gathering in Tiananmen Square, smashing any ideas of a right to freedom of assembly. On April 5, Mao Zedong issued a decree that stripped Deng Xiaoping of all his positions inside and outside the party. He was allowed to keep his party membership, but only so he could be monitored. Deng had been deemed the behind-the-scenes stage manager of the April 5 Tiananmen Incident.

When we saw the headlines in the newspapers, we were devastated. The only hope we had for China had been extinguished. All I could see was darkness. Where would China go? On April 12, I received a notice to go to Beijing for the shooting of a documentary, but I was not there in time to witness the protests in Deng's favor in Tiananmen Square. My friend Xiaoshan from the National Ethnic Song and Dance Ensemble secretly showed me a photo taken on April 4. He was standing in the Square, the Monument to the People's Heroes in the background, among a crowd of passionate people. They were listening to a speaker standing on the highest point of the monument. I could imagine the excitement. Thousands of Chinese people, who had suffered a decade of the Cultural Revolution, had come to the conclusion that this revolution was not as the leader had claimed it would be. Seeing this photo, which had not been confiscated in the police search that followed the Tiananmen Incident to prevent any evidence getting out to Western journalists, I understood I had missed something very important in the modern history of China.

Beijing, 1976: At Tiananmen Square in March, not long before the commemoration for Premier Zhou Enlai on April 4.

On July 6, Zhu De, the co-founder of the Red Army with Mao Zedong, died. And then, on September 9, we heard solemn mourning music from the loudspeakers. An announcer declared in a stern voice that our great leader, Mao Zedong, had passed away early in the morning.

Mao had left the world. It was impossible to believe—yet when the mourning music was broadcast, any sensible person would have known that, just like Stalin's policies had stopped the moment he died, it was the end of the Mao era. At that moment, I admit I felt great relief. An unhappiness that had accumulated in my heart disappeared. I was no longer the person who had "political black spots" and I ceased to feel the stone-like burden of my solitary confinement and the interrogations. I hoped this was truly a new dawn for me, and for all those Chinese people who had suffered for too long.

With the death of Mao, the Gang of Four faction—Zhang Chunqiao, Yao Wenyuan, Wang Hongwen and leader Jiang Qing— tried to formally seize the power they had been exercising in Mao's name during the Cultural Revolution. But they were loathed throughout the country. The division between Shanghai and other places became marked as three of the Gang of Four came from Shanghai, and our city was targeted for producing such hated extreme leftist figures. Political clashes extended to a partial embargo on raw materials going to Shanghai. In order to rebuild the city's relationship with Beijing and elsewhere, the Shanghai Revolutionary Committee tried to put on a stage show to tour other provinces and cities. We performers were to gather at the Friendship Cinema for training. On October 8, Xu Jingxian from the Shanghai Revolutionary Committee came to inspect our performance. According to the plan, after the show, all gear and costumes were to be packed and sent to the railway station. However, in the middle of the show, Xu said he was going to answer a long-distance call from Beijing, and he never came back. The show ended in confusion. What had happened? Without explanation, the tour was called off. In 2006, when I bought a book at Hong Kong airport called *A Dream of Ten Years*, written by Xu Jingxian after serving eighteen years in prison, I learned what had happened. "On the night of October 8," Xu wrote, "I went to the Friendship Cinema to censor a public show, and I purposely went there just to show my face. Then, after 8 o'clock, I rushed to Kang Ping Road, the study room for the Standing Committee Members . . . and I convened a counter-revolutionary military rebel meeting." In other words, he got mixed up in the turmoil.

One month after Mao's death, the Gang of Four were arrested, and their ultra-left ideological agenda suddenly came to a halt. There was a deafening roar of joy throughout China. Everyone wanted to celebrate the end of the Mao era, and now they were free to do so, even though they didn't know what was ahead.

Deng Xiaoping and his reform program returned from the wilderness, and people started to drink to the coming of a new age. I had always liked a drink, so I took the opportunity to have some with my circle of friends, such as the musician Gao Xiaoshan, photographer Wen Xiu, athletes Yao Lun and Yan Nan, and playwright Li Shoucheng. A lot of people spent their small savings on wine. Everybody in the street was happy. Mao had promoted the theory of class struggle, emphasizing the differences between people, which created a class hatred that replaced the sincerity, kindness and care which should be the norm in society. In the theory of class struggle, soft-hearted people would be eliminated first in each social upheaval. Those who were heartless and mean survived. The Gang of Four were nourished in such rich soil. After the Gang of Four had been overthrown, people started to think more freely. Why had Marx and Engels described socialism and Communism as beautiful when, in reality, the class struggle had been so cruel? People started to doubt Marxism and a crisis loomed that was beyond anyone's control, even the party's.

Meanwhile, I rode this wave of freedom, happily practicing my new skills in the belief that I would show them off on the national and international stage. The revolving platform is what it sounds like, and I soon realized it was very challenging. The platform created centrifugal force which made me dizzy and required extra strength to maintain balance and achieve my aim: an immobile sculpture of great strength and beauty, poised on one hand, on a revolving platform.

It was as if I had returned to the early days of my handstand training, being challenged to the extreme limits of my endurance. I had to face repeated failures. I was under pressure, too, as a lot of money and time had been invested in producing this platform for me. I understood, better than anyone I knew, that a person with great ambition must endure hardship, stress and loneliness on the path to achievement.

All of these efforts paid off when, in 1978, the revolving platform show went public. I received tremendous cheers from the audience. In that year I was thirty-one, an age when a performer in this art form was considered past his prime. Yet I achieved my goal, simultaneously dynamic and static, a motionless handstand on a platform in motion.

. . .

As I had anticipated, my achievement surpassed that of Ocinsky's. Over the next few years, my other achievements also surpassed Ocinsky's. I was able to execute a one-arm handstand while hopping up a flight of steps, and also a trick where I balanced on a series of bricks and knocked them away, one by one. Having two arms, I could do the inverted cross, an act taken from the sport of gymnastics, where you are suspended upside down with both arms extended horizontally. While gymnasts hang from rings, I balanced on a vee of two spreading poles. I could also do the iron cross, where you are suspended the right way up; the Maltese cross, where your body extends horizontally while your arms hold your weight; and the elbow planche push-up one-arm handstand, a variation of the one-arm handstand where you remain in a push-up position. What was unprecedented was I could do them all on our revolving platform.

I would have given anything to be able to personally express my gratitude to Ocinsky, as I had to Lauzik Malgit. Unfortunately, the relationship between China and the Soviet Union had gone sour, and we could not go back there. Yet again, politics had spoiled my joy.

Shanghai, 1978: My handstand on a revolving platform.
"Fight hard" is the number-one axiom in my life.

18

THE UNITED STATES

The historical clock had finally ticked over to Deng Xiaoping's opening-up and reform program. In 1980, the China Performing Arts Agency and Columbia Broadcasting System signed a contract for the Shanghai Acrobatic Troupe to go to the United States. This was the troupe's first commercial performance—as opposed to government-controlled diplomatic performances for political purposes—outside China since 1949. I had been the trainer in charge at the Shanghai Acrobatic Troupe school since 1979, but now I was hand-picked as one of the main performers, brought back to the main stage at age thirty-two when our country's prestige was at stake.

A presidential election was due in the United States. I hoped to learn more about it from the briefing before our trip, but an officer from the Shanghai foreign affairs office said only one thing about the election: "The opposition candidate, Ronald Reagan, is an ex-actor, and he wants to be president?"

During the training before the trip, I received a letter from a

classmate in Qingpu, who was undergoing a three-year labor rehabilitation program because of his homosexuality. His family were
KMT, too, and had moved to Taiwan. He hoped I would see members of his family if they came to visit me during our performances
in New York. I had not had much contact with this classmate, but
since he was in difficulty, I felt obliged to support him. In the past,
we had been strictly banned from private contacts outside China,
especially KMT. Now that we'd opened up and China had started to
treat people from Taiwan like compatriots, this rule had been eased.
I agreed to meet with his family and looked out for them when in
New York. But no one came. Perhaps things were not changing as
fast as I'd hoped.

We departed in April. After boarding the plane, I saw with great
amazement those who had boarded before us in the front rows: the
director, deputy director, the secretary of the delegation, other
leaders from the Cultural Bureau, a representative of the China
Performing Arts Agency and two stage managers. In the past, an
actor would take the role of the stage manager, but this time two
party cadres were appointed to do the job. There was one welfare
secretary and one actress, who had no performing duties but had
been approved by Wang, now fully rehabilitated as troupe director.
With so many cadres in the delegation, one more interpreter was
assigned. So there were nearly a dozen people traveling with us who
had nothing to do with the performances!

Our plane flew, via Tokyo for a one-night stopover, to New York.
April in Shanghai had already seen the arrival of spring, but New
York was still chilly when we got off the plane. The grand view of the
city from the sky was great, but when walking in the concrete jungle
I felt oppressed. With subway workers on strike, the traffic was
totally chaotic and had affected the ticket sales for our shows: not a
great start. However, New York is a city like no other in the world,

New York, 1980: Seeing the Statue of Liberty for the first time.

and on a Hudson River cruise, I looked out at the Statue of Liberty and recalled the refrain: "Give me liberty or give me death."

Standing on the top of the World Trade Center, I could feel the air floating around me. Looking down at a low-cruising helicopter flying among the buildings, I was reminded of Philippe Petit, a Frenchman who had come to our rehearsal two days before. He had walked on a tightrope connecting the two towers of the World Trade Center, 1350 feet above the ground. We professionals who had been in the trade for so long respected Petit's courage and balancing skills. His feat exceeded even the bravest I had seen, a female French performer who came to China in 1958 and showed a photo of her performing on a trapeze on a rope hanging from a helicopter.

Petit's great deed was not shown on television in China, but we heard of it through that unstoppable medium, word of mouth. We were told it was a fake: the imperialist countries paid huge money for an actor to pretend to risk his life. When we met with Petit, someone actually put that story to him.

He replied calmly: "That was propaganda. I just wanted to fulfill my dream. My friend and I didn't have permission so we pretended to be repair workers. It took us two weeks before we could install the fixed rope. The police only found out when I was walking on the rope. They lined up and pushed the onlookers back, and they took a helicopter up to ask me to go back."

He showed us some photos, one of which was of him walking on the rope, with his hair dishevelled and a helicopter behind him. What a great photo!

On the day Petit came to see us, a couple from Ringling Bros Circus who were practicing the handstand also visited. We took turns doing handstands. Some troupe members, looking at their performance, said, "They don't do handstands as well as you do, but they are paid more than you."

I remained silent.

In many cities around the world, there is a Chinatown. The first I ever went to was in New York. It was crowded with restaurants, herbal medicine shops and traditional craft shops. Walking there, I felt I was experiencing the struggle of a Chinese person in America. A tree may grow between two rocks, as long as there is a little mud there. The Chinese are the same. They can go anywhere, take root and develop.

At the entrance to Chinatown was a statue of Confucius, brought from Taiwan in 1974 when Confucius was being criticized during the Cultural Revolution. Long after his death, the two major parties in China were still fighting over him. Confucius was indeed a great man.

Even though we had our bureaucratic entourage, I was able to walk freely in Chinatown, and had a friendly chat with a student from Taiwan. "Rationally speaking," he said, "Taiwan should not be separated from China. However, in reality, you are so poor, and we are so rich, how could we be united?"

New York, 1980: The World Trade Center,
which still lives in my memory.

Prior to that conversation, I had attributed the lack of unity to political and military factors, and had never thought about the economic.

The second place we performed in was Atlantic City, famous as a gambling town. We stayed and performed within the hotel complex. During the long breaks each day between shows, we were allowed to go to the beach in small groups, or to see the casino, but we were not allowed to gamble. We had no money to gamble with anyway, and I had no interest. But I noticed how even though Atlantic City was in visible decline as a tourist resort, its gambling business was booming. People of all skin colors sat in front of poker machines and blackjack tables, gambling away what remained of their luck. From my observation, it was not money they were playing with; it was their fate, their luck, their nerve and the strength of their stomachs. Looking at these sad people convinced me of the truth of the saying "those who don't gamble are the true winners."

Seven days later, we boarded a bus to Philadelphia, birthplace of the American republic. When traveling, I loved to learn about the people, the history and the geography of a place, and enjoyed feeling close to major events that had occurred there. The first time I heard about Philadelphia was when the Philadelphia Orchestra had come to China not long after Richard Nixon's visit. Now I felt privileged to stand in front of the table on which the American Declaration of Independence had been signed, and to see the Liberty Bell. I felt like I was traveling through a tunnel in time, back more than 200 years, as I smelled the aroma of the print on the declaration, and heard the toll of the bell.

We received a very warm welcome from the Philadelphia Chinese community, who had prepared a magnificent array of dishes. But an embarrassing episode destroyed the atmosphere. Zhang, the deputy director of our delegation, was a Communist Party veteran, dating back to before 1949. He was affiliated with the Shanghai Opera

Research Institute, and had never had any dealings with our troupe. Who knew what connections got him on this trip? Zhang had a habit of drinking Chinese spirits, and was very often drunk on foreign wines, totally ignoring the foreign affairs rule that we were to drink no more than a third of our capacity. At the welcome dinner, Zhang, drinking heavily, slurred on about the highlights of his career, dumbfounding us by claiming he was friends with Gang of Four members Zhang Chunqiao and Yao Wenyuan. Afterwards, as we were waiting in the foyer for the bus to our hotel, the intoxicated Zhang rushed toward a young female performer for a hug. The scene became so chaotic, it was like a fox in a henhouse. The young girl was screaming, trying to avoid him. No one thought a poker-faced revolutionary deputy director could behave like this.

Philadelphia, 1980: The beginning of America's modern history. Here I am in front of the Liberty Bell with a young friend, and outside the building where the Declaration of Independence was signed.

In Washington, DC, while setting up the stage at the Kennedy Center Opera House, I looked at the box from which President Jimmy Carter would watch our performance, and reflected on how

Deng Xiaoping's opening-up and reform policy had made this trip possible. Just then, someone told me I was to be interviewed by a journalist from the Chinese section of the Voice of America. I asked, "What are the delegation's requirements regarding me talking to them?"

"Tell the truth" was all I got.

I found the two Chinese journalists in a corner of the dressing room, preparing their recording equipment and reading their notes. We introduced ourselves, and I was handed a piece of paper with their questions. I couldn't help thinking that, not so long ago, the Voice of America had been classified as the radio station of the enemy. Many people had been jailed and sent to labor camps for listening to it. I needed to handle this carefully, do a good interview, and at the same time not leave any loose ends behind in case the situation changed again in the future. After rehearsing my answers in my head, I said, "We can start now."

While one operated the recorder, the other fired away.

"Mr. Xue, how do you feel about the trip to America?"

"We left Philadelphia yesterday. I saw Independence Hall, where the 1776 declaration was signed, and I saw the Liberty Bell. I think it could be said that American history started in Philadelphia."

I avoided any questions about the problems and issues that had existed between China and America, and talked about the history of Philadelphia between 1790 and 1800.

"You are a main performer in the Shanghai Acrobatic Troupe. What is your monthly wage?"

"Sixty yuan a month."

I had spoken without thinking, and as soon as I said it, I felt something was wrong. If I was a main performer, then how come my monthly wage was not as high as the daily wage for a Ringling Bros performer? How embarrassing. So I added, "In China, we are implementing a system of low income and low costs. My wage is sufficient."

Luckily the journalist didn't ask what I meant by "sufficient." Nor did he ask any questions about the principle of distribution in China—"The more you work, the more you gain." I wouldn't have known how to answer, and it would have been very humiliating and potentially dangerous.

Half an hour before the performance in Washington, DC, when I was still preparing, I saw uniformed security guards with dogs doing a check. When the curtain opened, I saw President Carter and Chai Zemin, China's ambassador to the United States, sitting in the box. After the show, President Carter came backstage and had a photo taken with all the performers.

The Watergate building, not far from the Kennedy Center in Washington, DC, was famous for its namesake incident. Each day, as we entered and left the center, I'd have a look at Watergate. Like many Chinese, I was impressed with Nixon, as he was the person who turned a new page in the relationship between America and China, and laid a foundation for the new policy of opening up and reform. To those of us who had been through the Cultural Revolution, the Watergate political scandal was nothing. We couldn't understand how the American people could force Nixon to resign for "peanuts."

The tour in America had not been well organized and failed to attract large audiences. After the shows in Chicago and Minneapolis, due to financial losses, the American coordinators terminated the contract and canceled the shows in Los Angeles. We had to fly from Minneapolis via San Francisco straight back to China.

I met one person in Minneapolis who changed my life. Margaret Wong was active in her local community. Her Chinese-born father had been a high-ranking official in the KMT. In 1949, Wong's family

Washington, DC, 1980: President Jimmy Carter is in the third row from the front (center), and I am first on the left, caught in profile.

Washington, DC, 1980: In front of the US Congress, thinking about Watergate and its implications.

migrated to Brazil, and Margaret came to study in America. She didn't share the views of her father, who hated and held grudges against Communist China. She came to our performances thinking that no matter where we lived, we were all Chinese. She had been educated in the Western way and was very frank and open. Her American husband and two lovely children, and her American students who were learning Chinese with her, had all been influenced by her passion.

She took her family, her students and us on excursions. She invited us to perform in her Chinese school and to have dinner at her house. She added a lot of color to our days in America. That was the first time I had experienced the real life of a foreigner who was living comfortably.

One day before we left Minneapolis, Margaret said to me, "My husband would like to sponsor you to come and study in America. He asked me to seek your opinion. If you'd like to come, we'll look after all the application procedures."

Since China had begun to open up, some Chinese had gone abroad to study. Before Margaret made the offer to me, I had not thought about this for myself. I suddenly realized I was standing at the crossroads of my life. Coming to the United States to study performing arts would have a positive influence on my future career, and might also wipe out the fear that had been inside me since the Cultural Revolution. My enthusiasm outweighing my caution, I decided to accept her offer.

Minneapolis, 1980: It was time to leave America,
but I was at a personal crossroads.

19

SIDELINED

Not long after I returned to Shanghai, I received information about studying in Minnesota and the financial sponsorship materials from Margaret Wong and her husband. After obtaining approval from the troupe and the Cultural Bureau, and with documents issued by them, I went to apply for a passport at the Luwan branch of the Shanghai Public Security Bureau.

About one month later, my passport was posted to the troupe but was held back by the personnel department. I was then told that, following instructions from the Cultural Bureau, they had returned my passport to the public security bureau.

Later I found out that Mrs. Ma, deputy director of the Cultural Bureau, had intervened. When I went to see her, I waited outside her office for three hours, but she avoided me. I could not understand why a senior official would not take responsibility for her actions. Unable to see the point in meeting someone under her, I left. In the corridor, I met Tao Jiayun, who had been my superior when she was with our troupe during the Cultural Revolution, and had since been transferred back to the Cultural Bureau.

"Why are you here?" she asked.

"I'm here to see Mrs. Ma."

"What for?"

"I just want to find out why the bureau changed its mind about approving my passport application."

"I heard that it's because your sponsors are people you met during an overseas trip on formal business. That's why."

"Well, the personnel department told me the same thing, but I don't think that's a valid reason. When I applied to the bureau for permission to apply for a passport, they knew all of this. You know, a lot of government officials' children are studying in the United States. Since the Land Revolution War in 1927–1937, how many cadres of the Communist Party have had overseas connections? How many of those connections, especially those with the United States, could pass the internal party censorship? Of those people whose children are studying overseas, how many did not go as a result of connections established on formal business trips?"

While Tao stood there in silence, I kept unloading: "It is the new opening-up and reform policies that have made it possible for us to go abroad, and that's a right granted to us. To go abroad is to go abroad. It shouldn't be restricted to formal business trips, while private trips are not allowed. Also, while in the United States, I did nothing that would harm our national interest. When I came back, I did everything in accordance with the regulations. Why is it then that I can't get a passport?"

After hearing my long outburst, Tao patted my shoulder, shook her head and said nothing more.

After returning from the Cultural Bureau, I wrote two identical letters of complaint to the bodies in charge of passport applications: "According to the power endowed by the Constitution of the People's Republic of China, I, a citizen without any criminal conviction, have the right to obtain my personal travel document—a passport."

I was wasting my time. My letters were ignored. And then, using my inability to travel as a pretext, Director Wang removed me from onstage performances. I was devastated.

However, I could not accept that this misfortune was unalterable fate. I had lived through a time when we Chinese were taught to feel powerless, but it was human hands, not fate, that had thwarted me. The withholding of my passport was a clear message that even though the Cultural Revolution was over, the nightmare of dictatorship was continuing. The rigid political system had not been destroyed; the Communist cadres were still in power. Even though the country had opened up, the application for a passport by an individual was, in the eyes of those cadres, an act equivalent to divergence from the party.

The Cultural Bureau had cracked down on a wave of applications by individuals to go abroad. However, this only unleashed more unrest. The first troupe member to go AWOL during a tour of the United States, later than mine, was Meng Guiming. Meng's defection created a huge sensation. One of his mates in the acrobatic class, a student of mine, said, "Teacher Xue, Meng Guiming is—" He thrust up his thumb discreetly, meaning Meng had escaped. Then he said, "You should have stayed back in the United States. What could they have done to you?"

"I couldn't do that," I said. "Someone did talk to me about staying behind, and told me I'd have no trouble finding work in the United States and that they'd help me with the process. I told the person that I couldn't do that, as it would cause unnecessary trouble between China and the United States governments. Now the government is permitting individuals to go abroad, I thought I could take the normal channels and apply for it. I did not want to get involved in a defection. If I had jumped ship, the political career of the director in charge of the delegation would have been severely affected."

He asked, "You thought about them, but did they think about you? Aren't you suffering because of them now?"

I could not answer.

After Meng Guiming defected, more than twenty young performers from the Shanghai Acrobatic Troupe applied for political asylum during performance trips to the United States and Canada.

With my passport withheld, my stage life ended. The Communist Party had different ways of getting at you. Previously, they had simply put a political label on you or sent you to the countryside. In the new era, they withheld your passport or transferred you to a totally alien post and destroyed your professional opportunities. Between 1980, when I applied for a passport, and 1987, when I left the troupe, I was like an abandoned man. In my thirties, a mature age in our profession, I could do nothing. I yearned to be allowed to go back to the practice ground and the stage, but I was barred. I was like a fish that had been hauled onto the riverbank, panting for air. People say bitterness is a fortune. Maybe I should consider myself a wealthy man now.

*　*　*

My next six years of internal exile were a more prolonged and painful punishment than any of my sufferings in the Cultural Revolution. Back then, I was still young, with dreams of getting back to the stage and surpassing Malgit and Ocinsky. Now, I was finished as an acrobat. I still lived at the troupe compound in Shanghai, sharing a four-bed room with some young acrobats. All my possessions were in a slim single cupboard in that room. I ate in the troupe dining room. The rest of the time I read books, wrote letters, or went for long walks in the city. I was at least allowed to visit friends, who were angry about my situation; but there was nothing they or anyone could do.

It was called "soft punishment," but the passing of time was killing me like a guillotine or a firing squad. They had taken my job and my life. I wasn't even allowed to touch the acrobatic equipment. For any arts person, it is a hard time when you are past your performance years, but even the option of teaching was denied me. On just two occasions between 1980 and 1987, I had opportunities to teach—not because the authorities had come to realize their mistakes, but because they couldn't find anyone else.

In 1981, I was sent to the Ji'nan Acrobatic Troupe to teach them juggling with benches, an act where one acrobat lies on his back to support, with his legs, six levels of benches and three more acrobats above him. I threw myself into it with enthusiasm, applying the training methods I had used in Shanghai and helping to design the routines. I asked the stage designer from the Shanghai Acrobatic Troupe to design the gear and costumes. We started a very strict training program, beginning at six am with the handstand, followed by normal training. In the afternoon we focused on the show itself, and then, in the late afternoon, more handstands. I stayed with the performers all day, observing their every move. The repetitious practice did not bother the acrobats, who were keen for success. The show was a triumph, a result of their indomitable spirit and adaptability. They also had great confidence and trust in a trainer from Shanghai. The juggling with benches routine received a gold award in international competition. A rare bright glint in the darkness, this was an important moment in my teaching career.

In the autumn of 1983, the Anhui Acrobatic Troupe asked our troupe to provide two teachers for one month. Everyone else was busy again and even though it was not a sought-after position, I was delighted to go to Anhui and contribute to our trade. If I couldn't perform, I might as well teach.

Anhui Province had been stricken most severely during three years of natural disasters between 1959 and 1961; it also had China's largest numbers of deaths from starvation. Whenever people talked about Anhui, this topic would come up. A teacher from Anhui told me about a major conference held by the Cultural Bureau. An old lady who had suffered terribly was brought to the stage to help the audience "recall the bitterness of the past and enjoy the sweetness of the present," a pillar of the party's propaganda efforts. The old lady said that in the old society her life was hard, as the whole family went out begging, and they all lost contact with one another. In the new society, the government found and reunited her family. However, many of them starved to death in 1960. The audience started to whisper, so the party secretary took over: "You must be tired. Take a rest."

She was then escorted off the stage.

In another such session, at which I was present, we had to eat bran as a main meal. The propaganda teams holding the session told us that in the old society, working people ate bran. However, when the old people in the group said nothing, I was puzzled. I had fed pigs and knew bran was very coarse and hard to swallow. On that day, an old performer choked on the bran and passed out on the spot!

At a session held to demonstrate that corruption was the KMT's fault, a woman from a poor family was urged against her will to speak. "We are fishing people, living on a boat," she finally said after much prodding. "In the old society, we did not have enough to eat and wear. We were living miserable lives."

Her story greatly satisfied the workers' propaganda team. No one expected what she said next: "Well, life in the old society was harsh, but the new society is even harsher."

*1981: In a reflective mood on a boat on Daming Lake
in Ji'nan, the capital city of Shandong Province.*

*1985: When I turned thirty-eight, my birthday
wish was to maintain my positivity.*

She was recalling the bitterness of the past as well as the bitterness of the present! Since she was telling the truth, the whole audience stopped chatting and listened in silence.

A natural optimist, I wanted to live each of my days "cultivating my heart." I was influenced by the hero in *The Gadfly,* by the Irish writer Ethel Lilian Voynich. The strong-willed Arthur Burton, who has been tortured, takes little notice of the death that is inevitably in front of him. No matter what I faced, as long as I had the mental strength to pursue happiness, I would be all right.

One day, I had nothing to do, as usual. My life was solitary and idle. I randomly picked up the Shanghai Acrobatic Association newsletter, which had an article by Director Wang titled "The Diabolo Performer." It was a story about Tian Shuangliang, a street artist who had lived through the old and new societies. After he returned from Australia to China soon after the founding of the new China in 1949, a Soviet delegation invited him to view a movie, which so excited him that he shouted, "Long Live the CCP! Long Live Chairman Mao!"

The real story, I knew, was completely different. I had heard from a teacher, Shen Fangming, who had performed with Tian in Australia, that they went there together on temporary visas of eighteen months, and in 1950, when their visas were to expire, they were forced to leave. Unwilling to return to China, where the civil war had been fought and won during their absence, they tried to go to Europe but could not get a visa. They had no alternative but to return to China. Tian was worried the Communist Party would punish or even execute them for trying to defect.

Knowing this background, I wondered how he could have shouted those words about the Communist Party and Mao. So as not to mislead readers and to uphold the party principle of seeking the truth, I felt obliged to point out this discrepancy to the troupe director.

I took the newsletter to Wang's office and said, "Tian Shuang-liang did not shout, 'Long Live the CCP! Long Live Chairman Mao!' On the contrary, he said, 'Why are we going back? When we go back, the Communist Party will impose the death sentence on us.'"

I ignored the unhappy Wang's protests and continued, "This article may cause doubt in the readers. They may wonder why the Soviet delegation invited Tian to watch a movie. What movie was it? Was it Russian, or was it Chinese? At that time, shortly after the founding of new China, how many movies had China made? If it was a Russian movie, how could Tian, who understood no Russian and only a few lines of English, have understood it? And what caused him to shout, 'Long Live the CCP! Long Live Chairman Mao!'? Don't you think there is great contradiction in the logic here?"

Wang was speechless. His face changed from red to white and then white to red. I felt sadness, not triumph. We were still living with lies.

I was not scared of the troupe director. I clashed with him again on the day of the memorial service for a female lion trainer who had died of liver cancer. On the way back from the service, I thought about life and death, a law of nature that no one could change. Everyone is equal in the face of death. Death terminates everything associated with a person. The rich won't have their wealth anymore. The poor will no longer live in poverty. Those in power will lose control, and the weak won't be bullied anymore. Emperors and commoners will become the same. Death is like a reshuffling of life. Should there be reincarnation, one would come back to a different life and continue with a different fate.

As we sat in the vehicle, I heard Wang sigh, "Before too long, I will also go and see Marx."

To "see Marx" was a common way for party cadres to describe death, a pet phrase only for them. I couldn't help but confront him.

"You want to see Marx? Would Marx want to see you? Marx would want to see a socialism which is better than capitalism. Yet in the past few decades, what have you turned China into? Would Marx be happy to see such a society? Is this really what Marx had in mind? Marx said, 'I have sown the seed of a dragon'; but it turned out to be a flea. If Marx's spirit is up there, he would not like to see you."

Wang became very embarrassed and I felt bad. Why did I have to talk to him about Marx? I then laughed at my own naivety. I was losing my ability to remain silent, and it was always going to cost me, as long as I remained in China. It was now the end of 1986, and I had been sidelined from the acrobatic troupe for six years. Each day during those six long years, I had been thinking about how I could contribute. But management simply wouldn't give me the chance, and I was never going to give them the unconditional obedience they demanded. To go forward, I had to seek another path.

Paris, 1987: The Ji'nan Acrobatic Troupe's impressive juggling with benches won the Circus World Championships.

20

THE CALL OF THE SOUTHERN CROSS

I didn't want to yield to an unfair fate. That would be a waste of my life. Without any prospect of a job with the troupe, I hatched a final desperate plan: I had to get out of China.

For once, Heaven had decided to be kind to me: China and Australia had opened up for Chinese students. Sensing an opportunity that I couldn't miss, I enrolled in an English course in Melbourne and started the application process. By this time, Mrs. Ma, the person who originally took my passport, had retired. I got back my passport and went to the Australian embassy in Beijing to organize a visa. After that, I asked someone to help me buy a ticket to Australia. A friend of his, a man in Hong Kong named Zhang Zongkan, was able to do so if I sent him money. Once I got my student visa, which was surprisingly easy, I nervously posted my savings off to an address in Hong Kong.

I was like a timid rabbit, scared that anything could go wrong at any moment. Since the confiscation of my passport in 1980—even back to my detention in 1970, if I was honest—I had been living under a shadow of fear. People often say it is hard to leave one's homeland. But I was desperate. I couldn't endure any more, and staying in China only meant escalating anguish until the end of my days.

A few days after my ticket purchase was confirmed, I took my one suitcase, with my total savings of $150, to the Chinese side of the border with Hong Kong. I stood on the 50-yard-long Luohu Bridge in Shenzhen. Five yards under my feet, the river was running. It seemed to me that the clock had been reversed fifty years, to when a lot of overseas Chinese came pouring back to help construct the new China. However, many were labeled special agents of the enemy and even counter-revolutionaries, and many, with a broken dream and a broken heart, returned along this bridge to where they came from.

As I walked slowly over the bridge toward Hong Kong, and a totally different world, I thought about the insults the Chinese people had suffered from foreign powers. I also thought about all those political movements that had caused disasters for the Chinese. Why did our nation have to suffer so much? Well, I was leaving now. I shook my head and laughed at myself, in this shabby situation, still worrying about my nation and people.

When I got to the midpoint of the bridge, I stopped. One more step and I would turn a fresh page in a life which had been stalled for six insulting years. Those wasted years sharpened my yearning for freedom. If someone had put up a barrier, I would have run through it. I would have preferred to die rather than remain in that cage.

That's how I left China, where I was born and raised, and whose glory I had strived to enhance. I felt deeply sad, but my human dignity was more important now. Making a new life would take a while, but as long as I kept walking, I would be creating a path of my own. As I took a deep breath, I heard in my head:

There are no supreme saviors
Neither God, nor Caesar, nor tribune
Producers, let us save ourselves

Of all the songs to come into my head, it was the "Internationale"!
I walked to the other end of the bridge, toward my new life, and
new struggles.

*Hong Kong, 1987: A stopover on my flight to Melbourne. After the
turmoil and tragedy, my heart was as before, like calm water.*

On January 22, 1987, I boarded a Cathay Pacific flight at Kai Tak
airport and flew into the dark southern sky. The next morning I was
in Melbourne. I was forty, normally the time for the initial harvest in
life. But I was at a new birth, in a new country, a new man.

Alone in this strange place with no money, no English and a short-
stay student visa, I felt tremendous sadness as I watched the crowd
moving back and forth at the airport. A lyric from "Awaara Hoon,"
about destiny sending me away, came to my mind. I shivered.

I am but alone,

I am the destitute,

The world to me is like a desert

With no signs of life around

I am in no contact with anyone

I am like a star lost in the dark night

Roaming around

My destiny is so unfortunate

But I am not feeling sad

I don't feel sad at all

I hide my bitterness in my heart

And sing happily

Who can stop me from singing?

Oh, destiny, my destiny, my star

Please answer me

Why are you torturing me so relentlessly?

Survival was the first thing I was faced with. Where to live? What to eat? How to make money? I hadn't the faintest idea.

I had planned nothing, not even my first night's accommodation. My only thought was to get out of China, not what I would do next. I was placing my future in the hands of destiny. I knew the name of just one person in Melbourne. Before I departed, I had gone to bid farewell to some friends, one of whom, Xu Xibo, suggested I go to see a distant relative of his named Yuru, who had gone to Australia a few years previously. He said Yuru was a nice, down-to-earth person, a good girl. If I encountered any difficulties, I should go and find her. Even though I had endured a lot of hardship on my own, he said, I should understand the importance of seeking help in a new place.

Confused and concerned, I took my suitcase from the baggage

carousel and stood on the concourse outside, wondering what to do next. A Chinese-looking man approached me.

"Can I help you?" he said. "Are you waiting for someone to pick you up?"

"Nobody is picking me up."

"You look lost," he said.

"Do you know how I get to the city?" I asked.

"I can give you a lift, but what are you going to do then? Do you know anybody here?"

I said the only name that came to mind. "I know someone called Yuru."

In a lifetime of mixed fortunes, Heaven chose this moment to smile on me. The man, a restaurant owner named An Hong, knew Yuru—yes, the very same Yuru whose name and address I had been given in Shanghai. An Hong was at the airport to meet a friend, and once he had done so, he put us both in his car and drove me to Yuru's house. If I hadn't stumbled across An Hong, I still don't know what I would have done. The scenery outside the car was beautiful, but I did not pay it much mind; I just felt blessed to have met such a kind-hearted person. I looked at the sky and murmured a prayer.

We arrived at the home of Yuru and knocked at the door. When she first saw me, she paused for a moment, and asked, "Who sent you to come and see me?"

"Xu Xibo, one of your distant relatives in Shanghai. Even though he's much older than me, we are good friends. He said that if I had a problem, you would definitely help me."

She nodded. "Come in."

Yuru, who worked in a sewing factory, lived with her parents, who agreed to let me sleep in a spare room that first night. Yuru and I talked for some time. She seemed diligent, decent and reliable. The next day, I found the place in Hawthorn where my English course was located, and searched the local newspaper for a room to stay in. I found something in a three-bedroom share house in Church Street, Richmond, with an elderly woman and an old man who was a drunk.

I stayed at that house for three months, studying English. Yuru and I began to meet very frequently. Nearly every week, she drove one hour to Richmond and brought me fresh Chinese vegetables and greens like we ate in Shanghai. That warmed my heart.

She kept saying to me, "Everyone experiences hardship in a new place. After the initial period, a bright future will be waiting for you."

I didn't know whether that was true, but whenever I met with Yuru, I felt my sadness recede. We both came from Shanghai, then met under the Southern Cross. We found we shared a lot of things in common. Was this more of my old friend, destiny? I thought it must be.

To settle down and live in safety was the most important thing. Having left China, where I felt endangered, the urge to have a family of my own became strong. After some time, with the blessing of her parents, Yuru and I married. We moved into a rental house in Mooroolbark, in the eastern suburbs of Melbourne. Apart from the bed, our only furniture was two chairs and an industrial sewing machine serving as a table. This was how we started our life together, sharing bitterness and sweetness. I couldn't say we were able to live in comfort. But we had shelter to share, a place where we could help each other. We were not in love initially; marriage was an act of kindness on Yuru's part to help me stay in Australia. But after our wedding, like many couples in arranged marriages, we found ourselves falling in love. We were poised to enjoy safety, and a fertile, beautiful and peaceful life.

Now I was married, I did not have to be a student. I needed to find a job. Like most immigrants, I could not find a job in my trade—and jobs for acrobats were thin on the ground! Nor did I have capital to start up a small business. I had only one option: to find work on an assembly line. With a friend's help, Yuru and I both found work in a tile factory near our house. We chose the evening shift, so we could earn 15 percent more than on the day shift, and we could also squeeze in time to go to school to learn English. I completed another ritual of becoming Australian, which was to apply for and receive a tax file number.

Yuru quit her sewing factory job so that we could work together and come home in one car, a little compact Ford that we shared. In a big country like Australia, a car is a must. The work at the tile factory, with its corrugated asbestos roof and machines that were even older than me, was labor-intensive. Every week, I was paid $260 before tax. My initial job was to load the cooled tiles on the testing machine. Yuru packed the tested tiles into boxes. And then, my job was to check the flatness of the tiles. In summer, when the tiles had not yet cooled off, steam would rise off them and make me sweat all over. My work uniform got wet through—even my socks and shoes! This was another test of my will.

My work, simple and repetitive, was like that shown in Chaplin's *Modern Times*. I had to do the same task for eight hours every day, a total contrast to what I had been doing as a performer. My brain was not active, and my body moved along like the machines, numbed by the monotonous work. I could not see any future more exciting than this. All I could see was a machine.

I had been trained to live in suffering, and I had experienced it, socially and politically, which had left me with indelible memories but even greater determination. I could endure anything! If I was someone with no alternative but to work on an assembly line, at least I had something to do, unlike the previous six idle years.

Each morning, I went with Yuru to study English at the Mitcham Adult Migrant Education school, an investment in

*Melbourne, 1987: Me and Yuru at a party for Li
Shoucheng (right), author of the play* If I Were Real.

our future. I studied hard and finished all my homework, and the teacher noticed me. One day after school, the teacher asked, "Why do you work much harder than the students from Taiwan and Hong Kong?"

"To survive," I answered honestly.

Before going back to the factory for my late shift, I changed into my work uniform, to remind myself who I was and the role I needed to perform well. I imagined changing into a costume for performance and going on a stage. I hadn't changed. It was only the role that had changed.

The physical work developed my muscles. As I had back on the labor farms, I made the most of my situation and purposely trained specific muscles in my arms. Once the boring work had become part of my self-training, the hands on the clock seemed to tick faster.

Then an incident turned my life upside down all over again.

*　*　*

"The globe is not big, and one day we shall meet again," a Romanian-Chinese translator had said to me when we farewelled each other at Bucharest airport in 1973. Now, in a way, his words came true.

Focusing on work and study in Melbourne, I hadn't communicated with my friends in China. In September 1987, Li Shoucheng, a co-writer and performer of the well-known satirical play *If I Were Real*, came to Melbourne to attend the Spoleto Festival. Shoucheng, two years older than me, was a very handsome and intelligent actor and writer I had got to know in China. We had often met with his co-author Sha Yexin on weekends to discuss culture and the arts. Shoucheng had learned that I was in Melbourne. When he arrived, he searched for me through interpreters and friends but couldn't find me even after several days of trying. When he was having dinner in a restaurant in Chinatown, he let out a big sigh and said, "What a pity I can't get in touch with my friend Xue Jingjing."

Who would have thought that the waitress standing next to him was a distant relative of Yuru's? When later I heard Shoucheng's voice on the telephone, I immediately thought of the words of the translator in Romania. What a small world. I was delighted to see Shoucheng in Melbourne, and two days before the end of the festival, I accompanied him to an outdoor cocktail party. That was the first time I had the chance to meet with intellectuals in Australia. The atmosphere took me straight back to the old days in China, when I was still living the life of a famous acrobatic performer.

However, the get-together was short and I soon returned to reality. That glimpse of the arts world was like a piece of floating cloud. It appeared quickly and disappeared quickly. I must confess, I was a little sad to come back to earth. Bad memories came back to haunt me. However, at the end of 1987, Yuru and I were able to buy a house not far from where we worked. The asking price was $80,000 for the semi-rural cottage on a 8,000-square-foot block with a front and a back garden and good natural light. We bought it for $78,000. Yuru liked growing vegetables, and we planted flowers in the front yard. In the back we planted vegetables and fruit trees. I had always been interested in cooking, and before leaving Shanghai I had taken some lessons from a chef at the Jin Jiang Hotel. With the fresh veggies from my own backyard, I was able to cook delicious meals with the taste of nature, a different taste from supermarket vegetables. Back in China, when I was living in a small dormitory room, I had dreamed of having a house with courtyards. I had even thought of asking someone to do an oil painting for me, of a window from which I could see the backyard of this fantasy house. Now I had it for real.

Life in the new house was quiet and good. I lived my life according to a routine. In the morning, in the backyard, I practiced qigong, a traditional Chinese breathing and meditation exercise that helped me absorb the energy of nature. In the evening, I enjoyed the serene darkness, ridding myself of thoughts about the boring physical labor of my work. I looked at the stars, letting the breeze brush my body and take away all my worries.

The first time I looked at the stars, I was in grade three. Our teacher at the orphanage, Shi, took us to Penglai Park one evening and allowed us to lie on the lawn, which didn't have much grass, and look up. I was fascinated. Shi taught us how to identify the Big Dipper constellation, telling us that we humans lived on the planet Earth, a small planet in the solar system, which itself is a tiny, tiny part of the infinite universe. Listening to Shi, I thought of many questions. Will the twinkling stars fall down? Where is the edge of the sky? All this seemed so mysterious to me. Later, I got into the habit of talking to the stars, and found them to be the best listeners to my stories of sad experiences.

Those nights in my backyard in Melbourne, I felt the genuine beauty of the world. It was through this kind of meditation between heaven and earth that I relaxed my mind and purified my soul.

After I closed my eyes to sleep, I lost this balance. Dreams are out of our control. One frequent nightmare was of being detained, and the never-ending questioning sessions. The other one was that my brown Chinese passport was flying around me but I could not get hold of it. Then Mrs. Ma from the Cultural Bureau appeared between me and the passport and said harshly, "I have retained your passport. What can you do?"

"Why can't I have my passport?" I pleaded. "It's against the constitution that you confiscated it. Didn't you say we are the host of this country, and you are the servants of the people? Is it right for the servants to confiscate the host's passport?"

Mrs. Ma laughed. "And you believe that? How stupid are you? You believed whatever we said."

Melbourne, 1995: Meditating and contemplating heaven and earth.

With these words Mrs. Ma, and the passport, disappeared.

I would wake from this nightmare to find myself in my bed, in my house in Melbourne. It would be dark and quiet outside, with the occasional breeze stirring the leaves. Even though the nights were so peaceful, the dictatorship of the proletariat came across the ocean and two continents to sink its claws into me. I was living in Australia, a land of plenty, had a secure job, had Yuru to accompany me through everything; and the most important fact—I had my freedom. These were all gifts in reality, and as I came to realize that, I started to feel better.

Friends helped me get rid of the negative thoughts. In China I had often received support from my friends, so I tried to help those who came to Australia after me. My friends felt like family, and Yuru and I developed a circle we called the "Five Families." We all came from China, with similar social and educational backgrounds. Yang Guosheng, who worked at RMIT, had met me while helping my friend, the author Sha Yexin, when he was in Australia. Yang introduced me to Cherrie Zhu, who worked at Monash University, and Wu Yunji, who worked at Melbourne University. Soon, Yang's friends became my friends too. We helped each other, and I benefited a lot from this circle. Through my English classes, I made two friends from Hong Kong and Macau, who told me a lot about their lives there. Over weekends, I invited friends for a drink and a meal. Or we went out to a barbecue. Sometimes we went swimming, to enjoy the sun and the water, the green grass and the woods. Nature always relieved my stress. I was thankful to be living in Melbourne, a garden city, with so many gardens in the suburbs—truly one of the most liveable cities in the world.

In 1989, Yuru and I began working at the factory of a big truck company, with better pay and conditions. My job was to spray an undercoat on the bottom of the spare parts, while Yuru's was to sand the body of the truck. For more security, I became an Australian citizen. I had a new hometown and a new home country, and I knew I would have a good future.

It was in this year that the Tiananmen Square protests took place. The Chinese government crackdown on the student movement on June 4 in the Square focused the world's attention on a side of China I knew only too well. The news was hard to watch. Before the Communist Party had taken power, it had encouraged the people to demand democracy and freedom from the KMT government. The student leaders in this new movement demanded democracy and freedom from the Communist Party, but they were doomed. During the protests, I was chatting with a veteran soldier from Taiwan who thought the Communist Party was going to crash this time. I didn't agree; the Communist Party seized power by force and it wouldn't allow such a movement to succeed.

I was right. The bloody crackdown on June 3–4, 1989, was a very sad thing for those who had expected to live better lives with further opening up and reform. They must have felt betrayed by their country.

*　*　*

The free world had its own tyranny, the merciless economic cycles of the capitalist system. In 1991, Australia's economy followed the world into recession and, as an unskilled worker, I joined the army of the unemployed. Luckily, there is a good welfare system in Australia and I spent one and a half years in the Adult Migrant Education school and TAFE studying English. Yuru and I were able to subsist. During this period, we got ten young chickens: three males and seven females. With green veggies in the garden and the ginger-feathered chicks running around in the backyard, my worries subsided; and we had an interesting lifestyle for urban people. The chicks grew day by day, and our backyard became more lively. Every day, after I came back from school, the first thing I did was open the pen. Setting the chicks free to enjoy the yard was an exciting moment, not only for them but for me. Each time I opened the door, birds flew in to eat the food left behind by the chicks. What a contrast. The worry-free chickens were eager to come out to enjoy the freedom, yet the free birds wanted to fly into a wooden pen. The three male chicks grew up into roosters and they crowed each morning, so we had to destroy them. But one yellow hen took the role of a rooster and "mated" with the other hens. I could not understand it, and we had to have it destroyed, too. But another black hen took over the role of the yellow hen, and I finally realized I shouldn't intervene in nature.

In 1993, the economy recovered and I found a job on an assembly line in a sweets factory, which lasted for six years. In those six years, life was stable, but like a glass of water, without color or aroma. Friends still helped the situation. In 1996, Peng Xiaomeng, my friend who had been falsely accused of being a counter-revolutionary back in the early 1970s, came to Australia as a visiting scholar. After visiting Canberra, she came to Melbourne and stayed at our house for a few days. She was the friend with whom I had had the longest relationship, and we had always been on good terms. Today, our relationship is something I treasure. Peng's visit brought back memories of the days when I was detained, which reminded me of how lucky I was now. And in 1997, I was so glad to meet Gao Xiaoshan again when he came to study for his MBA at La Trobe University. We were a similar age, and he had treated me like family in China. In Melbourne, I reciprocated, asking him to treat my home as his home. I loved having friends with whom I could talk about the past. Parts of it were painful, but it was our life, and none of us wanted to forget it completely.

21

A NEW GENERATION

Sha Yexin was the second friend from China to visit my house. We had befriended each other when we were both being targeted by the Cultural Revolution. In 1988, when Sha came to Melbourne, I invited him to our place on a Saturday. He saw in me a down-to-earth proletarian, educated by the Chinese Communist Party, who after much effort and struggle had now achieved something in Melbourne. He asked me, "In Australia, all you can do is work in a factory. Do you regret coming here?"

"I have no regrets," I said honestly. "I have only changed my way of living, and I think it is a worthwhile change."

But was it enough? By 1999, I had been in Australia for twelve years. I had a home and a peaceful life that most Chinese would envy. However, I hadn't achieved anything in my acrobatic career. Though I had a job that paid the bills, I wondered if I would ever be able to start doing the things I loved. I knew that Heaven always has something for those who are fully prepared. I kept preparing and waiting . . . but nothing came.

While I was studying at the Adult Migrant Education school, our teacher asked us to practice by reading one article in the newspaper each day. As a very traditional person, I listened to the teacher and, after leaving the school, kept up this routine. One day, during lunch at work, I read an article about preparations for a national institute of circus arts. It had received a major financial grant of half a million dollars from the Sidney Myer Foundation. A job was advertised. I realized that Heaven had made its delivery.

For years I had been searching for such an opportunity. Back in 1987, in my first year in Australia, I had traveled to Albury, the border city between Victoria and New South Wales, for a job interview at a small circus school, the Flying Fruit Fly Circus. I didn't get it. I had also been rejected by Circus Oz's training school at Port Melbourne. I knew that both schools had financial difficulties, but I applied anyway. Neither of them seemed to understand the high standard of Chinese acrobats. Twelve long years later, all my hopes were reawakened. There were butterflies in my stomach as I read the article. That lunch suddenly became very delicious.

I knew there must be hundreds and thousands of people, Chinese included, who searched hard for opportunities to demonstrate their professional ability in Australia. Language and culture were sometimes insurmountable barriers. When an opportunity came you had to grab it, as it could slip away very quickly. The next day, I called the institute to find out more about the job and secured an appointment. I started to prepare for the interview and thought of all the questions I might be asked.

On the day, I went nervously with my friend Cherrie Zhu to a building borrowed by the preparatory committee at Docklands, and met the director, Pam Creed. My first impression of Pam was that she was energetic and a quick thinker. She asked relevant questions and was very professional. She had single-handedly raised funds for the institute, leased training facilities and hired teachers to start short training courses. I had read in the newspaper about the first short course, which she had used to show the Department of Education the necessity for and achievability of such an institute. I saw a very determined, capable woman.

What did she think of me? Well, I told her about being the main performer at the Shanghai Acrobatic Troupe and the trainer in charge at the Shanghai Acrobatic troupe school, and presented certificates showing that two of my students had achieved gold awards at international circus competitions. She listened to my not-so-standard English. I had Cherrie with me to help when I couldn't explain myself well. After seeing my resumé and video, Pam said it was fortunate for Australia's circus industry to have such a high-level coach from overseas.

After the interview, Pam invited me to have a look at the training ground, and asked me if I'd like to participate in the next week's teaching. I was overjoyed! If I had a week teaching there, I could easily determine the capabilities of each student, get a sense of the level of the Australian circus industry, and show them my skills. I understood that this trial was mutual.

At the close of the trial week, I received good feedback. A female student told Pam that she'd practiced handstands for ten years, but no one had ever told her that her weight was not spread evenly: it was on the tops of her palms, rather than spread across the whole palm. I asked her to shift her balance by moving her elbows and shoulders forward. In a week, I helped solve a problem which had troubled her for a decade.

Pam offered me the job. In 2000, I quit the boring and strenuous work at the factory, took off my worker's uniform for the last time and joined the teaching staff at the National Institute of Circus Arts. The moment I left the factory, a thrill of liberation came upon me.

I was confident I would do well because of my passion and my undaunted dream to continue my career by training young Australians.

In 2001, after one year's preparation, the National Institute of Circus Arts (NICA) at Swinburne University was founded in Prahran. I could do what I really loved. I was very excited, as it had been twenty-one years since I was last on the stage. I hadn't been practicing properly in those years, so how far had I fallen behind? I asked myself a serious question: Had I lost my capabilities? And how could my past experiences be of use today? What new skills would I need to learn?

At fifty-four, my physical abilities had inevitably declined. I was more than twenty years out of practice. I wondered what I would need to do when faced with young students with cultural backgrounds so different from mine. I still had to improve my daily English, and also the English used in my profession. With all these worries, I focused on conquering each difficulty one by one.

Knowing that the specific English terminology for acrobatic maneuvers would be the number-one problem for me, I wasted no time in learning it. In the institute, the ten trainers came from China, Russia, Britain, France, Argentina and Australia, so we helped each other. They helped me with language and the use of computers, while I shared with them my skills and experiences. Looking back, I still feel extremely lucky to have entered that environment.

Apart from English, I needed to build up my physical strength. I had to be energetic in front of the students to demonstrate correctly, protect them and gain their trust. No patient would believe in a doctor who was often sick. All those years working on assembly lines, I hadn't been wasting my time. When holding and passing stacks of tiles, for instance, I treated them as dumbbells. My arms were still strong. Now, I formulated a set of exercises which included handstands, somersaults, and waist and leg movements.

Melbourne, 2001: At fifty-four, I undertook daily practice to build and maintain my physical strength.

With practice each morning, I quickly regained my confidence and my musculature.

Our students were year 12 graduates who would undergo three years of training, which I thought was not enough if they wanted to fulfill their dreams on the international stage. But these students had backgrounds in circus, gymnastics and dancing, a great advantage for them. I wholeheartedly threw myself into the goal of training a young Australian student to outshine the rest of the world in circus arts.

Australia had proven itself at the Sydney Olympic Games a year before. With a humble population of 19.2 million, Australia's medal count was just behind that of China, a country of 1.3 billion. Athletes perform in similar ways to acrobats, with strong will, eruptive force, stamina, flexibility and strength. There was no reason our acrobats couldn't excel on the global stage as our athletes had done.

I started my students with the basics, and allowed them to choose the performances they wanted to tackle. The basics, such as handstands, somersaults, and leg and waist flexibility exercises, were hard and repetitive. After a few days, some students complained that they had practiced too many handstands and their arms and shoulders were sore.

I asked, "You stand all day long, and yet why don't your legs feel sore?"

They were puzzled about this and asked why.

"You have practiced walking and standing from the day you first walked, and you have just started practicing the handstand a few days ago. Of course you will feel sore. With more practice, you won't feel sore."

Other complaints came up later. Because they didn't enjoy handstands, somersaults and the flexibility exercises, some students said they just wouldn't choose routines that required handstands, somersaults or flexibility. I totally understood this concern because I had been through it myself. It was time to make things clear to them!

"When practicing anything," I said, "one must start with the basics. Acrobatics is no exception. Let's take the handstand. It improves the strength in your arms, and more importantly, it helps to develop your balance, which is of utmost importance in any acrobatic maneuver. Balancing is the core skill!"

I went on to explain flexibility, describing how a glass bottle smashes to pieces when dropped, while a plastic bottle doesn't. The key is the flexibility of plastic. The reason to train the legs and the waist is to improve overall flexibility so as not to get hurt. Now I could see approving nods and understanding in their eyes.

The training progressed better once the students understood the reasons behind what we were doing. After three months, it was time for them to choose their trainer and their performance. In that year, I had three students, all from different streams, all diligent practitioners, who I taught according to their physical condition, interests and needs. They all achieved good results after the first year, and one student received a scholarship for the second year.

Inspired by the students during training, I adapted a show that was purely technique-based into a performance called "Toy Boys," which was a lot of fun, and allowed the boys to demonstrate their strength. The students—boys and girls—showed me that with time

Melbourne, 2001: Explaining moves to students.

and proper training, they could become young stars on the international stage.

In the year I joined the institute, each trainer was required to say a few words to the new students. I said something along these lines: "The establishment of this institute provides a great opportunity and conditions for the cultivation of highly talented artists. All of you should treasure this opportunity and practice hard, as someone among you could one day go to international circus competitions and win gold medals."

The students all looked greatly surprised.

"Definitely. As long as you work hard," I assured them in a firm voice.

By the end of my first three years, I hadn't yet trained any Australian student to become outstanding, and I sometimes questioned whether I would. I wasn't sure until Emma Henshall appeared.

Melbourne, 2002 and 2003: My students training and performing at the institute.

I first met Emma in 2003, when she took the short course. She was only sixteen at the time, a pretty girl with a strong figure and big bright eyes, but a little shy. With many years of dance training behind her, she was confident and had excellent artistic charisma in her every move. Emma studied at the institute between 2004 and 2006, and became the best student I had ever taught.

Emma chose trapeze to be her performance, even though in her enrolment tests she could not do a single chin-up. So why did she choose trapeze? Much later she told me. She had consulted the head trainer, who told her she couldn't possibly do trapeze as she didn't have any background in gymnastics. It turned out that Emma just needed to prove someone wrong. She was quite sure that with proper training and practice she would achieve her goal.

That was the kind of spirit I liked. It was how I had achieved my goals: if someone said I couldn't do something, that was all the motivation I needed. Creativity stems from a strong will and self-confidence. I could see this belief in Emma, her conviction that anything was possible, so I agreed to her choice.

In many ways, by coaching Emma I was able to revisit the stages of my own development in China—to go back through my life, no less. She found the beginning torturous, growing tired and bored with the hard daily drills, hurting herself when she didn't do the right moves and hit the iron rod on the trapeze, and getting bruises all over her body. Every day, she would be faced with failure, and her disappointment was obvious. Her knitted eyebrows accompanied her sighs.

I saw all that, and tried to show Emma that, to become a good acrobat, all of this was inevitable. "Everyone who has just started to do these exercises experiences exactly what you are experiencing, feeling depressed, stressed and frustrated," I told her. "But those people who really want to achieve something will get through these

Melbourne, 2004: Emma Henshall and me.

things eventually. It's a ladder. After conquering each obstacle, you will move to one level higher up. Those who are hit with these difficulties and give up are not the ones who can be successful. If you want to be successful, you have to continue facing these setbacks. The sweat, the tears, the hurts and the wounds are the price you pay for success."

I might not have said the above things in perfect, logical English, but Emma understood. She soon emerged from the shadow of disappointment and started practicing with a smile.

I hoped that Emma would have such a happy mood every day when she came to the training hall. But I had to hide my keen expectations. Even though there were imperfect moments, I could not show too much disapproval, as I didn't want to discourage her. I wanted to show her the duck above water, gliding elegantly, not my feet paddling like mad under the surface.

Training Emma was as much a learning process for me as for her. I couldn't just replicate my experience; I needed to create methods suited to her talents. She had the special individual charisma of a Western acrobatic performer, and I hoped to merge that with the techniques that Eastern performers are good at, so she could have the best of both worlds. This was an opportunity for both of us, but I always bore in mind that I needed to carefully design a training schedule for her and her alone.

Emma was not afraid of difficult and dangerous moves. On the contrary, she took them on as fun. That was what made me realize she had potential to go to international circus competitions and win gold medals. I started to encourage her to set an international gold medal as her grand vision. She accepted my professional opinion, and that drove her through much hardship.

From the moment Emma set this goal, she found herself to be time poor. The schedules set by the institute for the three-year course only allowed students one hour a day, five days a week for training in their chosen performance. In that hour, a lot of elements needed to be covered. How could so little training time be enough for the cultivation of an international performer? Unfortunately, the institute could not afford more hours for the trainers.

It would have broken my heart if Emma, such a wonderful marble, was not carved into a great artwork. I had to find a way to break the problem of time limits. But how? By increasing the "density" of the training? No. I had put so many elements into the allocated time, Emma seemed to be close to her physical and mental limits. Maybe I should try to optimize the elements she practiced—increase the actual difficulty? We decided to abandon the traditional training sequence for a hybrid program, which included some basic training and some complex movements. After some trials, it worked. I increased the level of difficulty gradually while checking if it improved her performance. I didn't want to increase the level of difficulty just for the sake of it.

I also gave my own time. One of my colleagues asked me how much Emma was paying for the extra hours of training we inevitably needed. I smiled and didn't reply. We had very different ideas about value. What he was interested in was the income. I was more interested in achievement. The happiness that resulted was beyond any monetary measurement.

Safety was paramount. I had suffered a lifetime lesson, a chronic right knee injury due to the absent-mindedness of a safety guard in China. I didn't want anything like that to happen to Emma. Each time before training, I ensured that all safety gear was in place, that Emma was fully focused and that, before she did any moves, I was by the protective wire. Because of all of these precautions, Emma had no accidents during the three years we worked together.

I liked to encourage her with success stories from history. I told her about Beethoven's piano on which the ivory keys had been dented by practice; about Gai Jiaotian, the famous Peking Opera performer who, after the doctor had wrongly set his broken bones, deliberately broke his leg again. Along with these success stories, I shared my years of experience. I told her how I found a stronger vitality in life when I challenged my failures. I also told her how I felt on top of the world, in every way, when I set the record in handstand.

* * *

During the Christmas holidays in 2004, I went to Ji'nan for a holiday. I went around like a tourist, quite happy to observe the booming economy, the many new buildings and the visible improvements in how people lived.

I visited the deputy director at the Shandong School of Arts in Ji'nan, who was also a handstand performer. He took me to the practice ground and introduced me to two young acrobats practicing the pyramid chairs on a spinning platform. "This is Trainer Xue," he said, "whom I have always mentioned as a famous acrobatics trainer from Shanghai."

I was touched that my name was being mentioned like that, given that I had been absent from the performing stage for twenty-four years. Later I learned that these acrobats went to Moscow in 2005 and two of their performances included skills created by me. Also, they used gear of mine which had been passed down. Not long after I came back to Australia, I learned that their pyramid chairs had won the international gold medal, and was extremely happy that my artistic life had been extended in China. I told Emma all this during our breaks because I wanted her to know how very special it feels to succeed at the top level. However, I didn't tell her about the political environment in which I achieved all of this.

During the 2004 Olympic Games in Athens, an Australian female diver, Chantelle Newbery, won a gold medal after being trained by a Chinese coach. One Australian colleague joked to me: "Only Chinese coaches like you with no-good English can train Olympic gold medalists."

I laughed and said, "When training an athlete, you don't need great speeches, just clear, concise words with the correct message. Those Chinese coaches with no-good English actually have very good experience."

My colleague understood that pretty well, but he asked a further question. "Why don't they stay in China to train athletes there?"

I told him that in China at that time politics was more important than the coaches' skills. Their expertise would not be taken seriously if they did not toe the political line, and, furthermore, their behavior would be considered disobedient. All they could do was go into self-imposed exile and come elsewhere to seek opportunities.

My colleague shook his head and seemed not to understand. He hadn't lived in a society where knowledge and skills were considered suspect. He couldn't comprehend why capable people would go to a totally strange place and risk losing everything.

At this stage, Emma was growing distracted by other opportunities. I told her a story about a bear with some corn. The bear picked an ear of corn, and held it to his chest. He picked another one, but dropped the first one. He went on picking, but he kept dropping the previous one. In the end, he only had one ear of corn, the one he had picked last. I think Emma was very impressed with this story and understood what I wanted to say. I often found that a story, a saying or a sentence was more powerful when said at the right time, during breaks or at the times when she was down or losing focus.

In her second year of training, Emma's overall abilities improved and she began designing and creating a performance that was uniquely hers. When performing, she displayed the skillfulness of an artist, and she had reached quite a high standard technically. Most importantly, she had a gold medal in her heart. One delicate issue came up. Emma told me that quite often she was on the receiving end of bad language from another girl in the class, which annoyed her. All outstanding people will encounter envious behavior from others who are not as good. I had experienced a lot in my career. In China at the time when I was performing, envy often turned into hatred. That was something I could not do anything about, which made me feel helpless. I explained to Emma, "The fact that others envy you suggests that you are better than they are. You should be proud of this fact. The best way to deal with that kind of behavior is to ignore it. Concentrate on your practice and training. The best form of counterattack is success. Do not even think about those who envy you, for they are not your competitors. It is as simple as that."

I also checked the dictionary for the word "envy." It gave two meanings: envy and admire, and envy is a result of admiration. I showed this to Emma, and that helped clear her worries. In the 2005 Christmas card she sent me, Emma wrote: "Dear Jing Jing: I have never before had a coach with such a strong spirit and belief in his students. I thank you for your patience and wisdom, gifts which I know are rare and valuable."

In her third year, Emma could perform a pirouette on the trapeze with great ease. She had climbed one mountain after another, and was on the way to the highest mountain yet. She had paused, stopped and been defeated at times, but she persisted. I had been trying to find out the reasons for the small setbacks and solve those problems, finding better ways to cultivate good talent. How I treasure those three years of exploration.

Melbourne, 2005: Emma in training.

Emma was now in sight of her goals, but unfortunately I could not take her to the international stage and see her pick up a gold medal. She had finished the institute's three-year course. She chose to go to Canada to make the last dash toward her gold medal. For me, the departure was hard, but I strongly believed she would succeed, and she also understood that in the faraway southern hemisphere, there would always be a pair of eyes watching out for her. In 2008, Emma sent a DVD from Montreal to show me her training. She rang and told me she would take her trapeze routine to the international circus competition in Paris. I was ecstatic, but also worried about whether she would be able to perform at her usual level under competitive stress. Compared with other performers from China or France or other countries, Emma lacked international experience. But I could not voice my concerns. I only said, "When at the competition, just remember two words: 'I can.'"

Opportunity is there for those who are ready, and Emma was ready. In January 2009, she won the gold medal for her trapeze act at the thirtieth Festival Mondial du Cirque de Demain, the premier international circus competition, held each year in France. Pam Creed called me from Paris the next day to break the news. This was the first time an Australian performer had won an international circus gold medal. She did it. She succeeded.

Soon after, Emma called to say she was going to sign a contract with Cirque du Soleil. Hearing her excited voice, I said very happily, "Congratulations on your successful competition."

"Congratulations on your success, too."

"Pardon?" I didn't get her meaning.

"My success is your success. That's why I want to congratulate you on your success."

Emma was a very understanding girl. She knew I had great expectations for her, but didn't let them weigh her down. She did all the training not only for herself, but for the fulfillment of my expectations; and, when she was successful, she didn't forget me. That greatly touched me. I looked up at the Southern Cross and said proudly, "I now have someone to carry on my career."

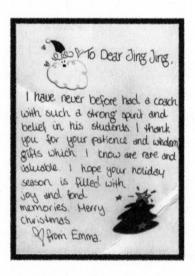

Emma's Christmas card, 2005: A written message from another person had seldom made me happier in all my life.

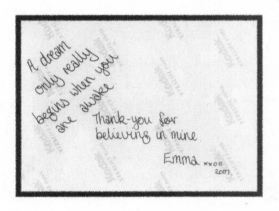

A note from Emma, 2007: A dream only
really begins when you are awake.

Melbourne, 2009: Sharing the happiness over her medal win with Emma at the National Institute of Circus Arts.

22

EVERYONE NEEDS
A DREAM

Emma spent five hard years achieving something few could imagine, let alone do, in their entire life. Her gold medal inspired other Australian acrobats to follow her path. In May 2009, she came to Melbourne for a one-month holiday and, instead of relaxing, asked me to help her with an even more difficult task: swirling in the air during her trapeze act. Within one month, we unlocked the secret. Emma's resolve to break through to greater heights was more precious than a gold medal and I sincerely felt so proud of her.

As a teacher from China, I felt very lucky to be able to teach at NICA. It was a rare opportunity to share my Chinese roots with Australian youth, and combine the east with the west. Cultivating students and turning them into stars like Emma added great meaning to my life. However, such students were not easy to come by, despite my active search.

In 2011, when I was sixty-four, I started to plan for my retirement. I still felt that there was something unfinished in me, but did not know where to start. Just when I was about to give up, two new students caught my eye: Liam DeJong and Tamika Jade. From the outset, they demonstrated outstanding qualities: strong bodies, quick responses, strong will, brave spirit and abundant energy. They also had extra qualities needed for the international stage—beautiful figures, handsome faces and bright, expressive eyes. Tamika had previously studied dancing, and it was quite easy for her to learn the handstand and somersaults. Her dancing training gave her the ability to achieve perfect acrobatic poses. Liam had excellent technique, explosive power and good balance when holding weight. I saw, more importantly, in both of them, the inner determination to pursue their dreams.

I was keen to train them, and they chose me from among several candidates who could teach their chosen performance piece, adagio. This is a very difficult combination of partner throwing and catching, along with formations. They would need perfect harmony in movement, rhythm and expression. I could see their questioning eyes, asking: "Can you fulfill the promise given by the institute and turn us into international-level acrobats?" I gave them a positive answer: I had confidence in them, but they had to commit to this goal. During the next three years, I said, they must not be content with a graduate certificate. The audience couldn't care less about what certificate they had, only what they did on the stage. They would need to put in a lot more effort than others.

They would experience many difficulties, especially Tamika, the person being thrown up in the air and coming down. Liam needed the strength and skills to catch her before she landed on the ground, or on him. Actually, Liam was hit many times, but he held onto her. Tamika, when landing on Liam, would also feel pain. But neither complained much. The similarity of their personalities meant they could be trained and shaped well. My passion was reignited.

The first barrier was once again the lack of scheduled training time. The institute, to prevent too many similar performances from their students and also the possibility of over-intense competition, required that each student must have two hours of classes each day, and each class must be different from their performance area. But the students knew how to work the system. Liam and Tamika chose acro-balance as their elective, to fulfill the course requirements, but used the class to strengthen their foundation for adagio. Even with such an arrangement, the two-hour training each day was still not enough.

As I had done with Emma, I tried to make up for these limits by raising the requirements in their basic training. I asked them to per-form each move as if they were competing on the international stage already. It was difficult for me to design something that was perfect for them and also beautiful and grand enough for the international stage. We were all under pressure. Liam and Tamika gave up their holidays and weekends and came to the institute to practice hard each day. The three of us were like competitors against time, work-ing for our common goal. When I looked at their exhausted, sweating faces at the end of each training session, I understood we were one day closer to success.

Inevitably, they experienced failures, which diminished their morale. I often asked questions to get them thinking. Liam was a power-type acrobat, and I asked a simple question: "Who do you think is stronger, man or tiger?"

"Tiger."

"Then why do tigers go into the cage? Why don't the strong tigers get men into the cage?"

"Eh?"

"The major difference is that man has the ability to think. To achieve something, you need to think. Ask 'why' about everything you do in training."

The question they asked often was, "What is your secret to success?" They were so keen to succeed, and needed a role model.

"To do better than all people in my generation in my trade," I replied. "I had that in my mind all the time. It was like a fiery torch that lit up my whole struggle. Especially when I was low and down, the torch was something I looked up to. It drove away my darkness and made me see the bright future."

"Why in the seventeen years you were performing in China could no one surpass you?" they asked.

"Because I never allowed myself to become content with my situation, and I dared not dwell on the successes I had had. I always looked for a breakthrough or an improvement in myself. Only by pushing myself forward was I able to stay in the lead. At the same time, my peers were happy to follow in my footsteps and they chose not to become creative and find their own way to success."

The last sentence was said especially for them. I had noticed that the students at the institute collected a lot of material from TV, the internet, DVDs and magazines about trends in our industry. I tried to guide Liam and Tamika not to imitate what they saw, but to keep questioning. How did this acrobat do something with such a level of difficulty so beautifully? What are the norms behind all those elegant performances? What they saw on the videos was the past tense for those performers. "If you imitate that," I told them, "you'll always fall behind. But, if you analyze how they did it, and you learn the method, it will help you with your 'future tense,' using your creativity. I want you to do something original, that belongs to you. Find your own path. Remember this."

Our training continued in a happy atmosphere, and they improved rapidly. In 2012, they had to not only follow their usual study programs but also prepare for a stage performance in September. I fast-tracked their physical strength programs to get to a

*Melbourne, 2011: Shadowing Tamika and Liam
during their training to protect them.*

level where they would be able to undertake the full performance.

This acceleration produced difficulties. In winter, Tamika, who hated the cold, had to endure it. Liam was not a great fan of the heat, so summers were hard for him. After some adjustments, they were able to bear a lot more than they thought they could.

When practicing a new move, they both became frustrated by their initial inability to master it. When first learning the pirouette catch, Liam was not able to see the quick one-and-a-half body pirouette Tamika was making in the air. He said it was impossible for him to catch her.

"Yes, it is possible," I said in a firm voice. I explained that this was normal. "Don't mind that at this stage, and don't feel frustrated by it. The most important thing for you is to endure it, and calm yourself down. To endure may seem negative, but actually it is a very positive part of practice. You must endure each failure until one day, after practicing it every day for many days, you will do the move, and you will catch Tamika in the air. And at that point, you will understand that the most valuable characteristic of training is to endure, to make yourself patient. In your daily training, if you control your unsettled heart, you will find success beckoning you."

Tamika and Liam were able to endure. By August, they had built up their physical strength to the level required, and their technique on the moves was close.

For first-time performers, nerves were inevitable, and to overcome them would also take time. I remembered when I was little, before going on the stage, the teachers would look at us with stern, cold eyes. They saw all my mistakes and punished me with their harsh words. My seniors were punished physically. Such punishment only makes performers more nervous: we would feel the punishment for mistakes even before we appeared onstage. As a teacher, I used a different method. I told Tamika and Liam to have confidence in their ability to control their movements on the stage like they did in training. They were nervous out of inexperience, not a lack of competence. Upon hearing this, Liam and Tamika grew more able to manage their nerves. When the actual performance came, they were at ease in front of the audience, and their performance was a success. I felt so proud of them. The institute granted them full scholarships for their study in 2013, which made me even happier.

In October, Emma came to Melbourne for a holiday. I asked her to come along to see Liam and Tamika's training, and on Melbourne Cup Day I invited all three to my house so that they could share their experiences, and especially so that Liam and Tamika could feel the energy and happiness emanating from a winner. I hoped they would be inspired by Emma, who talked with touching honesty about her training, the hardship, the

Melbourne, 2012: Tamika and Liam had
the determination to endure.

Melbourne, 2012: Tamika and Liam's performance was a success.

breakthroughs, the international competition. She genuinely hoped they could emulate her; she radiated an infectious aura.

When we started to eat, they complimented me on my cooking. I chose not to say too much about my past; I never wanted the weight of my experiences to affect my students or weigh them down. So I told them that when I was young, I liked good food very much but was too poor to go to restaurants too often. I learned to cook to satisfy my own stomach. I understood that their routines were stressful, I went on, but they should learn to cook to give themselves a treat, as a reward for their endurance in training.

By 2013, Liam and Tamika had started to practice the pirouette with Tamika rotating her body 720 degrees in the air—two full rotations, when a year before Liam said they couldn't manage one and a half! During a break in November, we had another of our usual "dialogues." Tamika wrote down "impossible training possible," and asked me to translate those words into Chinese.

"Most audiences will think what you are going to do is impossible," I explained as I wrote down the Chinese characters. "However, it is our task to make it possible. The difference between possible and impossible is the mark of distinction between performers. Those who think it's impossible will never be successful. Those who think it's possible will be favored with success. The means of transforming the impossible into the possible is training—long, hard training—nothing else."

Liam looked at the words: "impossible, training, possible." He wondered why he was now able to do a cartwheel push-up one-arm handstand, when the technique trainer had once told him it was impossible. I said, "Training. Your previous trainer's comment was a result of his own limitation."

Next, Liam wrote the word "endure" and asked me to do the same thing. This was one of the words I most frequently used during their training. "Endure" had a special meaning for Liam and Tamika. I spelled it slowly, e-n-d-u-r-e, and then asked what the meaning was in English. They said it meant "to tolerate." I told them that the Chinese character for "endure" has two parts. The part on the top is the edge of a knife, and the part on the bottom is a heart, and these vividly explain the meaning—if you can bear the edge of a knife on top of your heart, there is nothing you cannot tolerate.

Later in November, at their graduation performance, Liam and Tamika exceeded their usual standard and won great applause from the audience and teachers, who realized that in such a short time and using the institute's schedule, outstanding talents could be cultivated.

I rushed back from the staff Christmas lunch in a restaurant to finish their last day of training. Afterwards, they brought out a small box and said they had a Christmas present for me. I opened it. It was a pair of very delicate pens with engravings on them. One said "Impossible. Training. Possible." The other was the Chinese character for "endure." I looked at their eyes, full of respect and love. I nearly cried.

The year 2013 was another harvest year for me. Liam and Tamika's adagio laid a foundation for them to go on to the international stage. I also received a DVD from Emma showing her work with Cirque du Soleil. Watching her perform, my heart filled with pride. I remembered her words: "My success is your success."

But as I knew, the world is not a perfect place. At the end of June, Swinburne University had announced that Pam Creed would leave NICA. The news came suddenly, and we would never learn the true reason behind it. Pam had devoted all her passion and energy to the institute from its inception through every stage of its development. Whether building the new training ground or preparing the training curriculum, and recruiting teachers from all over the world, Pam had spared no effort. She was the founder and real heart of the institute. After establishing it, she tried her best to raise funds, applying for government grants and realizing the plans to build a new circus center, interior drama room and a movement room. In 2007, she invited the then federal treasurer, Peter Costello, to the opening ceremony of the new national circus center, which was good publicity for the institute.

Pam's sole mission had been to contribute to the development of Australia's circus industry. A petition to get Swinburne University to revoke its decision was circulated and I put my name to it, as did most of the teachers and students at the institute. In the end, Pam was transferred, but the petition proved her popularity.

There was another incident. During the 2013 graduation performance period, in the section about Tamika on the board "Cast of 2013," three names appeared as her trainers, and my name was last.

What had happened? I asked Georgia, who was in charge of marketing and promotion. She told me the descriptions were provided by the head trainer, who had put two more names down for Tamika's trainers. Liam and Tamika graduated at the end of 2013 with high distinctions. They wanted to participate in the international circus competition in Paris in 2015, but three years of training was not enough to prepare them sufficiently. They didn't want to have to go to another institute, as Emma had. They performed in front of NICA's new director, Rose Stephens, after which Tamika told Rose that they wanted to go to the competition representing the institute. "If we do that, would NICA consider extending our training for one more year?"

Rose thought for a moment and said, "What if other students also have the same desire?"

I chipped in: "Other students should be encouraged, as this would create a positive competitive atmosphere, and this would be helpful in lifting the standards of the students."

Rose said, "I think it is reasonable to request the increase of training time for the international circus competition. I shall consider it, but I need time to make some arrangements."

At the beginning of December, all students received an email from Rose saying that those who were capable of participating in international circus competitions could apply for an extension of time for training, but the maximum would be three months. Three months was much shorter than the one year we had asked for, and due to my teaching load I could only squeeze in one extra hour for Liam and Tamika per day. It was the best we could do, and the three of us had to work extremely hard.

In February 2014, when it was scorching hot in Melbourne, we were at the last stage of our three-month training. I hoped to spend another six months of unofficial training with them. I was quite confident that as long as there were no safety or injury issues, they would succeed. However, at one training session at the end of March, only Liam showed up, looking extremely stressed.

"What's happened?" I asked.

Liam said in a hoarse voice, "I broke up with Tamika. No more adagio."

"What?" I was shocked. "No chance to reconcile?"

Liam shook his head. I understood that was the end of it. These inseparable lovers separated, and at the same time gave up their dream. I tried to believe it, but I also tried not to believe it. Liam and Tamika fell for each other on the training ground, and the sparkle of their love was as brilliant as any fireworks. This young couple had generated huge power out of their dreams. However, love is like a double-edged sword; it can also destroy hope in a split second.

This unexpected turn of events actually taught me another lesson in life. A successful acrobatic performer must endure pain and hardship not only in training, but also in their outside life. One should always expect the unexpected. I must confess this incident was a big blow for me, as I would not be able to present another good result to the institute at the time of my retirement. I kept on with my life, kept dreaming my dream. If I could meet with more promising students, I might postpone my retirement again, and give it another shot. The past thirteen years had given me such joy.

At the end of 2014, Tamika signed up with a circus company called the Han Show, based in Wuhan, China. She didn't even need to do an interview. She simply posted the videos of her training and performances and was accepted. Liam took up a position as a coach in a sports club in Melbourne. They had started as individuals and later formed such a close relationship that they had become one entity, but now they'd gone their separate ways. It was a pity, but what they had done would be remembered, and I had no doubt that it would be a driving force in their futures.

23

GO FORWARD!

During Chinese New Year in 2015, I received a present from Emma, who was in America: a poster of Cirque du Soleil signed by all members of the troupe. Emma had written on the poster: "You are the best coach in the world. You changed my life and have been such a positive influence!" Actually, it was Emma who changed her own life. I only shared with her my experience, my ethos and my own way to success. The success was hers.

People like to compare things. They compare babies to see who is cuter. They compare students to see who studies better. They compare adults to see who is more successful. They compare the elderly to see who is healthier. It seems people live their lives engaged in comparison. In my own life, I had stuck to my principle of not looking up, not looking down, not looking back and not looking around. I had my goal and I always looked ahead. I maintained the principle of never complaining, but knew I needed to struggle against unfairness and suffering. Complaining about life is not the answer. In order to make life more meaningful, one must look for hope, most of all in miserable times.

From my first one-armed handstand performance in 1963 until

1980 when I finished my stage performances, no one surpassed me. I was absolutely determined to be number one. I taught the performers in the Ji'nan Acrobatic Troupe the art and skill of juggling with benches, and they won two gold medals; I coached Emma and she eventually won an international gold medal—a first for the industry in Australia. These three events lit up my life, which has been full of setbacks and hardship. I feel my efforts could withstand close scrutiny from anyone, even if I have to do a "struggle session" in the afterlife.

If I were asked, "What is the meaning of life?" I would say it is not reflected by the amount of wealth one possesses, but by the value one creates. The biggest question is, have you made the most of your intrinsic capacities? No matter how unfair life was to me, I held to this belief. I have had many desires during the different stages in my life. Now, the one in front of me is the erection of a plaque at the institute saying "Go forward," in the hope that more young performers will be inspired to find their way to success.

* * *

There is one final episode I wish to talk about. I have been putting it off, as it is so painful to recall. It happened when I had reached the end of the road with the troupe in Shanghai and was considering a future outside China. This was the episode that finally tipped me over the edge and led to my coming to Australia. It revolved around the most sensitive questions of my existence: Who are my parents? Where did my ancestors come from? What happened to my family? Why did they abandon me?

These thoughts had been with me every day, causing heartache, frustration and sadness. As a child at Fuyou Orphanage, I would look at the gates every day and hope that my uncle, my mother or father, or someone else from my family would walk through, lift me up and take me home. I may forget the orphanage buildings, but I will never forget the shape and color of those thick wooden gates, opening from the center, covered in peeling black paint.

After I joined the acrobatic troupe in Shanghai, my wish grew into an expectation. I envied those classmates who had parents visit them on Sundays, and those who received letters from family. But I told myself that the greater an acrobat I became, the more my fame would spread, and one day I would look into the audience and there, among the seats, would be my mom and dad.

In bed on sleepless nights, I tried to picture what my parents looked like. *They must be handsome. Do I have siblings? How many? I am not a bossy boy, so I am probably not the eldest. Are my grandparents still alive? What uncles and aunties do I have?* I had no way of finding the answers to these questions. I could only shout helplessly in my heart: *Mom, Dad, where are you?*

In 1984, I started trying to find my parents. As I had got older, the desire to find them had intensified. Contrary to their usual sluggishness, the bureaucracy acted quickly, finding an original newspaper record in the Ministry of Civil Affairs: Xue Jing, born in 1947 in the Fenghua district of Ningbo, Zhejiang province, sent to Shanghai Fuyou Orphanage in 1950. I discovered that Dong Bin, the then director at Fuyou Orphanage, had died in prison in 1954. I had not expected this basic information to come so easily, so I was encouraged to dig deeper.

Those records were consistent with the only piece of information I had ever gained, from the librarian who was then working at the Youth Village. He had received me from my uncle at the Fuyou Orphanage. I had visited this man, named Wang Ying, with my classmate Wang Lisong in 1955. Ying said he could only remember that when my uncle left me there I was about two or three. He couldn't tell me my parents' names. As Shanghai people like to use double names for children, my name Jing had become Jingjing. That was as much as he could remember.

In 1984, Wang Lisong, who later became a teacher at the No. 3 Primary School in Dongjiadu Road, and I took a bus to a farm in Zhenru on the outskirts of Shanghai, to visit Dong Bin's wife, in the hope of finding more clues. When we arrived at the farm, we saw an old lady in rags, with a worn apron around her waist, standing by the pig pen. The wrinkles on her forehead were like knife scars. Her hands were like the bark of a pine tree. In Shanghai in April, we were in spring clothing, but she was still in winter clothing and trembled from the cold. Were it not for her pair of bottle-thick glasses, which marked her as an intellectual, she would have looked just like an old farmer's wife.

I couldn't believe my eyes. The Mrs. Dong I remembered had been dressed in a cashmere coat with light makeup on her face. After finding out what we wanted, she invited us to her home, a place she shared with one pig. That is exactly what the Chinese character for "home" depicts: a pig under a roof. It was so sad to see where she was living. The stink was unbearable.

She said apologetically, "If I had known there would be visitors, I would have done some cleaning up. And I haven't got anything to offer, not even water."

We apologized that we hadn't contacted her in advance. Wang Lisong was older than me, and while I sat there in shock he talked with Mrs. Dong about life at the Fuyou Orphanage. I looked around and suddenly remembered—I had been here before. When I had pneumonia in the orphanage, Mr. Dong had been afraid that I might pass it on to others, so he brought me here. But later he changed his mind and took me to the Renji Hospital, which saved my life. At that time, the death rate for pneumonia was high. If I had not been sent to the hospital, I might not have survived.

Mrs. Dong was well educated and, after some pleasantries, explained that as she only went to the orphanage once in a while, she didn't remember much about me or my background. She wished her husband was here to help me, but he had died in prison after being arrested for rape in 1951. She protested her husband's innocence: at the memorial ceremony, she said, the alleged victim had cried; Mrs. Dong wondered why she would cry her eyes out for her rapist. The girl was a mute orphan who, Mrs. Dong said, Mr. Dong had really cared for. On the way back from the farm, Wang Lisong told me that not long after Dong's arrest, Fuyou Orphanage became a public primary school.

I shifted my hopes to Fenghua, my birthplace. Fenghua is also the hometown of Chiang Kai-shek, the president of the KMT and brother-in-law of Song Qingling, who was made honorary president of China in 1981. I hoped that the people who were around Song Qingling would know a lot about Fenghua. So I asked a good friend, Zhan Che, an actor with the China Welfare Institute Children's Art Theater, to make some inquiries for me. Song had known Zhan Che for many years, and her secretaries were very friendly with him; he often visited them. He promised he would try.

One Sunday morning, Zhan Che took me to 369 Shanxi North Road, and knocked on a door of a three-story Western-style building with high bamboo fences. Zhan told me that this house had belonged to Song Qingling, who later gifted it to a few of her secretaries. Zhan received a warm welcome from one of the secretaries, who listened in silence to my questions before answering: "In Fenghua, there is no Xue family. From what we have just heard, we think your family may have changed your surname. This is all we know. We suggest you go to Fenghua to find your parents and family."

Zhan needed to stay and work, and I was escorted to the main gate. It was a quiet Sunday. The person seeing me off, a deputy secretary at the China Welfare Institute, said, "Young man, how I wish it was this quiet when the Communist cadre are giving a talk."

I nodded and smiled. I remembered how queasy I felt when listening to the big talks given by the cadres.

The next morning, I went back to the civil affairs department and told them I had met with Song Qingling's secretary, who suggested I go to Fenghua to try my luck, and I officially sought approval to travel there. After some discussion, my request was approved. The department even sent a young assistant to accompany me to Fenghua, with the troupe taking care of all expenses. On the ship to Ningbo, I relived the memory of coming to Shanghai. The boat was swaying from side to side, my uncle was holding me and I was crying and vomiting.

This memory strengthened my resolve to find my parents. As we approached Ningbo, my heart beat faster. I would find my true family, see my parents, look at them, find out their age, their health, their occupation, and probably my siblings, my grandma and my uncle. Would my uncle's wife be beautiful? How many kids did they have? All these questions, which are nothing to normal people, obsessed me.

After the ship docked at the Ningbo port, we boarded a long-distance bus to Fenghua, which turned out to be a beautiful little town. We checked in at a guesthouse, ate and went straight to the police station, the public security bureau, to seek assistance. The bureau issued some reference letters addressed to its branches in the region. In the next few days, we traveled the area with the reference letters, checking one branch and outpost at a time, asking if any families by the name of Xue were there. There were but two Xue families in the region, and both had arrived there in recent years.

I made contact with these two families, but they said they hadn't sent any of their children to a Shanghai orphanage, nor had they heard of anyone in their family doing so.

During these travels, I strained to recall what my family looked like. I remembered my maternal grandma lived in a two-story house. She had a shrine with a statue of the Buddha. Grandma burned incense three times a day and prayed to the Buddha for peace. On festivals, the whole family made offerings in front of the shrine.

I could also remember eating popcorn in my grandma's house. I can still see children surrounding the popcorn machine with their hands over their ears, waiting for the loud bang when the popcorn was done. Cheerful laughter followed the crack, and Grandma would clap together two wooden fish to signal that we could eat.

But without an address, these memories were in vain.

Even though the search was unsuccessful, I went to the county public security bureau to thank the police. They told me that usually it was the parents who set out to find their child or children. There was no precedent for a child looking to find their family. Without a correct family name, the most critical clue, it would be very hard to find them. I hadn't realized that a change to my family name, which now seemed likely to have taken place, would bury my past. Perhaps my family had been determined that I would not be able to find them. But why would they abandon a two-year-old boy? The Chinese had always attached great importance to boys. There must have been some major disaster in the family; otherwise, my parents wouldn't have done this. I had survived much misery since I had been abandoned, but I didn't blame my parents. I trusted that what had happened must have been outside their control.

On the boat back to Shanghai, I looked up toward the stars in the dark sky. I asked, "Where are my roots? Why does everyone else know about their roots, but not me?" There was no answer. And this search ended like a shooting star. Once again, after a moment of hope, my origins fell back into the darkness of the unknown.

I did get something from the search. Through the librarian, I had found out that my name, Jing, meaning "compete," was the name truly given me by my parents. It felt like it was their hope for me to compete and survive in the cruel world. Looking back on my life, I had always competed and had never given up, even in the most difficult times. This one word, Jing, linked me to my parents.

ACKNOWLEDGMENTS

BEFORE CHRISTMAS 2007, PAM CREED told me: "Jingjing, it is time you wrote your autobiography. I am sure Australian readers will be very interested in your story." I said to myself, my autobiography will not only include my career in the acrobatics field, it will also include every aspect of my life in China and Australia. When I told my relatives and friends at our Christmas party at home that year, all agreed I should go ahead with the project. They wanted me to take the matter seriously. And they urged me not to wait until after my retirement before I started.

I didn't know where to begin. It was time-consuming to re-collect information from 1949 to the present, and to achieve an accurate record of those matters, people and events. I wanted to write about many things that had happened in China, but in Australia I had limited means of checking information. I also hadn't been in the habit of writing a diary, as that would have left concrete evidence for the persecutors in the Cultural Revolution. That was a wise move then, but not so wise now! I was lucky to be in contact with my classmate Zhou Yanji, who lent me her diary of our African trip.

I hadn't used a computer before, either, and I needed to overcome the primary barrier, typing Chinese on it. To do that, I needed to learn the official Chinese phonetic system, starting from A, B, C. The most difficult part of writing the autobiography was to put my thoughts and memories into words. I had never written these things down, and I had no idea how to write thousands of words. Over the years, I wrote and rewrote the words and sentences over and over again.

I would like to thank my relatives and friends who have encouraged and helped me. Wu Yunji and Cherrie Zhu read my manuscripts and provided many comments and suggestions. Chen Qingping scanned all the photos I wanted to use. Song Zheng provided me with a lot of guidance in using the computer. It is with these people's help and support that I was able to bring this autobiography to you. Without them, I don't know how I could have done this, as I would have had to, as the saying goes, "feel the stones in the river and cross it."

I must thank the following people for bringing this book to life. Thanks to Bo Ai, the translator, and to Mavis Clifford and Edith Wilson, for proofreading. Bo Ai and Edith were recommended by Yang Guohen. Mavis Clifford was recommended by Bo Ai, as they both taught for a period at RMIT, and have worked together on other projects. The English version of this book is the result of several years' hard work by Bo Ai, to whom I would like to express my special gratitude.

This book includes some photos from my past, to help bring to life the people and the stories. Because I have been living in Australia for years, it is a pity that some sources of the photos and the photographers who took them are no longer identifiable.

To all those people who have helped me in my life, especially in the low times—in the orphanage, in detention during the Cultural Revolution and the six years after that—I want to say thank you. It is you who have given me warmth in life, and made me feel the true good nature in people. I also want to thank those who persecuted me, or assisted in the process. It is they who made me hold my head high and wield my strong will.

ACKNOWLEDGMENTS

It is my wish that all people, and especially those in China, might live with dignity. Those disastrous years of the past, like a page of history, have been turned over, and I hope they will never come back.

Last but not least, I thank my wife, Yuru, for everything.

THE TECHNIQUE OF HANDSTAND

ON THE EVENING OF MAY 1, 1963, on the eastern side of the Tiananmen rostrum, a young acrobatic performer named Xue Jingjing was preparing for his handstand against the strong 5-6 grade wind. His final act was to perform a one-arm handstand on a pole, with eight timber rings being maneuvered by his legs and his other hand. In such a wind, the timber rings could be blown away. Some well-intentioned people became concerned, and suggested he cancel this item. However, Xue Jingjing said in a very firm voice, "I can. I definitely can do it well." So, with the wind as the accompanying music, Jingjing did it, and he did it successfully.

The basic skills needed for acrobatics are waist, legs, somersaults and handstand. Handstand is the most important skill. In the many performing items, extra moves are added to the basic skill of handstand: for example, standing on top of a stack of chairs or a pile of bricks. The hardest one to perform is a single-hand handstand. There are very few performers who can do this.

After liberation, the overall performance level of the handstand in China was greatly improved, and Xue Jingjing became one of the top performers of this act. In 1960, when he first followed his teachers to perform abroad, he read in a magazine about a Hungarian acrobat, Lauzik Malgit, performing a single-hand handstand on a pole. One of the photos showed Malgit performing a single-hand handstand on a pole, with four timber rings being maneuvered by his legs and other hand. That was described as the world's best handstand. Many people regarded it as impossible to surpass, but Xue Jingjing didn't think so. With the encouragement of his coaches, and with his own tremendous effort, a few years later, Jingjing was able to do the same, only better, as he could maneuver eight rings, setting the highest standard in the world. He also created the one-arm handstand block drops and, in the 1970s, he created and performed the one-arm handstand on a revolving platform.

It is a great honor for me to write in tribute to one of the most talented circus performers the world has known. His talent has pushed forward the level of attainment possible in the handstand, and in circus. But this is not the sole reason I am proud to write about Jingjing. He is a pillar of strength in so many ways: in his dedication and ambition, in his loyalty and sense of fairness and, with fondness I say, in his kind heart and understanding.

I know all of these things because he was my coach.

Jingjing has the ability to make you work hard, with repetition and also laughter. He did not have to punish me or be forceful and strict because he simply commanded respect and I soon understood that my dedication to the training was the best thanks I could offer.

I remember the happiness of training under the instruction of Jingjing, and the immeasurable depth of knowledge he has.

He taught me more than circus; he gave me tools for life. And best of all, in the true spirit of Jingjing, he taught me to use those tools not only for ambition, but for kindness and understanding. I extend my endless gratitude to him, for his unwavering belief in my ability and future success.

Emma Henshall
United States, December 3, 2012

GOLD GLITTERS
EVERYWHERE

ALL ACROBATIC PERFORMERS KNOW HOW difficult it is to perform a handstand. To do it on one arm is even harder. In the 1960s and 1970s, Xue Jingjing from the Shanghai Acrobatic Troupe was one of the best. He was able to perform a single-hand handstand with eight rings in his other hand and on his legs. He represented the Shanghai style of acrobatics, which left a great impression on all who saw it.

Before Xue Jingjing, performers in China only performed two-hand handstands. He was the first person to be able to do this in China, creating a national record.

How did this come about? There is a story. In 1956, the Shanghai Acrobatic Troupe went to Europe for a friendship performance trip, to Romania, then Eastern Germany, Poland and Hungary. At that time, I was only sixteen years old. I remember we were warmly received. During the six months we traveled, we were showered with flowers, applause and laughter. One unforgettable moment happened in Hungary. It was so long ago that I can no longer remember the performer's name, but we all referred him as the "Little Moustache."

One night, he performed a single-hand handstand with four rings, and his performance won the praise of the audience. He was an accomplished performer in Hungary, and his wife told me, "In order to prepare for his act, he spent several years training himself, only taking time out to eat and sleep. His success didn't come easily." The success of "Little Moustache," Malgit, had also been noticed by Zhang Guochu, the director of our delegation, who was then in charge of the Beijing Cultural Bureau. In one of the meetings we had, Zhang encouraged us by saying, "Whoever can do the same handstand as that Hungarian acrobat will be an accomplished performer in China."

The secretary to our delegation, Liu Jintang from the Shanghai Acrobatic Troupe, expressed the wish that such a performer be from his troupe. After that trip, many took up the challenge, but for various reasons, all failed until 1963 when Xue Jingjing became the first person to bring that act to the stage in China. Xue Jingjing, after coming back from his African trip, and strongly encouraged by one of his delegation members who also went to Europe with him, set his goal. He used different methods, and he applied different theories in his own pursuit of this move. He included gymnastics, ballet and acrobatics, and designed his own program for training.

In 1987, Xue Jingjing went to Australia. I met him when I went to Melbourne in 2007 and gave lectures at the National Institute of Circus Arts Australia, where he had been teaching for several years. It's worth mentioning that, in 2009, when I went to observe the international circus competition in France, the gold-medal winner, Emma Henshall, was his student.

Jingjing and I have been good friends for some time, and we often share our teaching experiences. I am very proud of his achievements in the acrobatic field, and I believe he is a piece of gold that will glitter everywhere he goes.

Lu Yi, former deputy chairman of the Chinese Acrobatic
Association, former director of the Nanjing Acrobatic
Troupe, artistic director of the San Francisco Circus Center
San Francisco, March 25, 2012